P9-EKS-809

Heavenly Cross-Stitch
Designs with a Christian Theme

Marie Barber

Sterling Publishing Co., Inc. New York
A Sterling/Chapelle Book

For Chapelle Limited

Owner: Jo Packham

Editor: Ann Bear

Staff: Areta Bingham, Kass Burchett, Rebecca Christensen, Holly Fuller, Marilyn Goff, Shirley Heslop, Holly Hollingsworth, Sherry Hoppe, Shawn Hsu, Susan Jorgensen, Pauline Locke, Barbara Milburn, Linda Orton, Karmen Quinney, Leslie Ridenour, Cindy Stoeckl

Photography: Kevin Dilley, Photographer for Hazen Photography
Photo Stylist: Jo Packham

We would like to offer our sincere appreciation of the valuable support given in this ever changing industry of new ideas, concepts, designs, and products. Several projects shown in this publication were created with the outstanding and innovative products developed by:

- **Anchor**; 30 Patewood Dr., Ste. 351; Greenville, S.C. 29615
- **Charles Craft**
- **DMC**; 10 Port Kearney Building; South Kearney, N.J. 07032-4688
- **Gay Bowles Sales, Mill Hill Beads**; P.O. Box 1060; Janesville,WI 53547; 1-800-356-9438
- **Krenick**; 3106 Timanus Lane, Ste. 101; Baltimore, MD 21244; 1-800-537-2166
- **Wichelt**; N 162 Hwy 35; Stoddard, WI 54658; 1-608-788-4600
- **Zweigart-Joan Taggart Ltd**.; 2 Riverview Dr.; Somerset, N.J. 08873; www.zweigart.com; email-info@zweigrt.com

Library of Congress Cataloging-in-Publication Data

Barber, Maria
Heavenly cross-stitch : designs with a Christian theme / Marie Barber.
p. cm.
"A Sterling-Chapelle book."
Includes index.
ISBN 0-8069-0349-X
1. Cross-stitch-- Patterns. 2. Christian art and symbolism. I. Title.
TT778.C76B38 1998 98-18737
746.44'3041--dc21 CIP

10 9 8 7 6 5 4 3 2 1

Published by Sterling Publishing Company, Inc.
387 Park Avenue South, New York, N.Y. 10016
© 1998 by Chapelle Limited
Distributed in Canada by Sterling Publishing
c/o Canadian Manda Group, One Atlantic Avenue, Suite 105
Toronto, Ontario, Canada M6K 3E7
Distributed in Great Britain and Europe by Cassell PLC
Wellington House, 125 Strand, London WC2R 0BB, England
Distributed in Australia by Capricorn Link (Australia) Pty Ltd.
P.O. Box 6651, Baulkham Hills, Business Centre, NSW 2153, Australia
Printed in the United States of America
All rights reserved

Sterling ISBN 0-8069-0349-X

If you have any questions or comments, please contact:

Chapelle, Ltd., Inc.
P.O. Box 9252
Ogden, UT 84409
(801) 621-2777
(801) 621-2788 Fax
chapelle1@aol.com

Due to the limited amount of space available, we must print our patterns at a reduced size in order to give our patrons the maximum number of patterns possible in our publications. We believe the quality and quantity of our patterns will compensate for any inconvenience this may cause.

The written instructions, photographs, designs, diagrams, and projects in this volume are intended for the personal use of the reader and may be reproduced for that purpose only. Any other use, especially commercial use, is forbidden under law without the written permission of the copyright holder.

Every effort has been made to ensure that all information in this book is accurate. However, due to differing conditions, tools, and individual skills, the publisher cannot be responsible for any injuries, losses, and other damages which may result from the use of the information in this book.

About the Author

Marie Barber, born and raised in Kristianstad, Sweden, now lives in Ragland, Alabama, on the Coosa River with her husband and their two children.

Marie says she has always loved to draw and illustrate. At the age of 14, she was the youngest student to study oil painting under the instruction of the late Dr. Göran Trönnberg.

She came to the United States in 1983 as an exchange student, and in 1987, returned after being accepted to the Art Institute of Atlanta. She has freelanced as a novel illustrator for a Swedish weekly publication and her artwork is featured at Loretta Goodwin's Gallery in Birmingham, Alabama. Although she has explored several avenues of the art world, Marie says she found her passion in 1993 when she began designing cross-stitch patterns.

Table of Contents

General Instructions 4
Cathedral Glass 7
Celestial Melody 12
Cherubic Garden 15
The Road to Bethlehem 21
Three Wise Men 24
Mary & the Christ Child 27
Jesus & the Children 31
Scenes of the Nativity 35
The Last Supper 43
The Lion & the Lamb 49
Noah's Ark 53
The Christmas Play 57
A Good Report 62
A Praying Child 62
Scripture Reading 65
Santa 66
Kids Count 71
Two by Two 75
Animal Angels 80
Puppy Angel 80
Squirrel Angel 80
Bear Angel 83
Bunny Angel 83
Kitten Angel 86
Angel & Baby 88
Morning Chorus 89
Family Tree 92
Little Red Church 94
A Christmas Sampler 97
A Floral Sampler 103
A Winter Sampler 109
A Bear Sampler 116
An Alphabet Sampler 122
Metric Conversion Chart 128
Index 128

General Instructions

Introduction
Contained in this book are 118 counted cross-stitch designs, including 90 miniature cross-stitch designs.

The mini-designs have been graphed in sampler form, but may be stitched either individually or as the sampler. Included for every design is a photograph of the completed work. However, photographs of some of the mini-designs are not included, in order to include as many graphed designs as possible. Each graphed design includes its own color code.

Fabric for Cross-stitch
Counted cross-stitch is worked on even-weave fabrics. These fabrics are manufactured specifically for counted-thread embroidery, and are woven with the same number of vertical as horizontal threads per inch.

Because the number of threads in the fabric is equal in each direction, each stitch will be the same size. The number of threads per inch in even-weave fabrics determines the size of a finished design.

Number of Strands
The number of strands used per stitch varies depending on the fabric used. Generally, the rule to follow for cross-stitching is three strands on Aida 11, two strands on Aida 14, one or two strands on Aida 18 (depending on desired thickness of stitches), and one strand on Hardanger 22.

For backstitching, use one strand on all fabrics. When completing a french knot, use two strands and one wrap on all fabrics, unless otherwise directed.

Preparing Fabric
Cut fabric at least 3" larger on all sides than finished design size to ensure enough space for desired assembly. If the design is used to embellish a project that will be finished further, check instructions for specific fabric allowances.

To prevent fraying, whipstitch or machine-zigzag along raw edges or apply liquid fray preventer.

Needles for Cross-stitch
Blunt needles should slip easily through fabric holes without piercing fabric threads. For fabric with 11 or fewer threads per inch, use a tapestry needle size 24; for 14 threads per inch, use a tapestry needle size 24 or 26; for 18 or more threads per inch, use a tapestry needle size 26. Never leave needle in design area of fabric. It may leave rust or a permanent impression on fabric.

Finished Design Size
To determine size of finished design, divide stitch count by number of threads per inch of fabric. When design is stitched over two threads, divide stitch count by half the threads per inch. For example, if a design with a stitch count of 120 width and 250 length were stitched on a 28 count linen over two threads, the end size would be 8⅝" x 17⅞".

Floss
All numbers and color names on the codes represent DMC and Anchor brands of floss. Use 18" lengths of floss. For best coverage, separate strands. Dampen with a wet sponge. Then put together the number of strands required for fabric used.

Centering the Design
Fold the fabric in half horizontally, then vertically. Place a pin in the fold point to mark the center. Locate the center of the design on the graph. To help in centering the samplers, arrows are provided at left-side center and bottom center. Begin stitching all designs at the center point of graph and fabric.

Securing the Floss
Insert needle up from the underside of the fabric at starting point. Hold 1" of thread behind the fabric and stitch over it, securing with the first few stitches. To finish thread, run under four or more stitches on the back of the design. Never knot floss, unless working on clothing.

Another method of securing floss is the waste knot. Knot floss and insert needle down from the right top side of the fabric about 1" from design area. Work several stitches over the thread to secure. Cut off the knot later.

Carrying Floss
To carry floss, weave floss under the previously worked stitches on the back. Do not carry thread across any fabric that is not or will not be stitched. Loose threads, especially dark ones, will show through the fabric.

Cleaning Finished Design
When stitching is finished, soak fabric in cold water with a mild soap for five to ten minutes. Rinse well and roll in a towel to remove excess water. Do not wring. Place work face down on

a dry towel and iron on warm setting until the fabric is dry.

Cross-stitch

Stitches are done in a row or, if necessary, one at a time in an area.

1. Insert needle up between woven threads at A.
2. Go down at B, the hole diagonally across from A.
3. Come back up at C and down at D, etc.
4. To complete the top stitches creating an "X", come up at E and go down at B, come up at C and go down at F, etc. All top stitches should lie in the same direction.

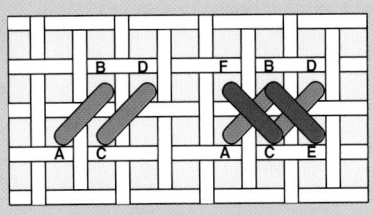

Backstitch

1. Insert needle up between woven threads at A.
2. Go down at B, one opening to the right.
3. Come back up at C.
4. Go down one opening to the right, this time at A.

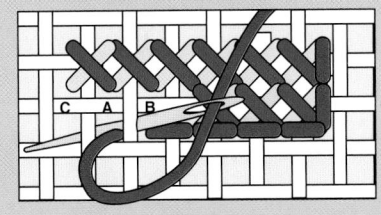

French Knot

1. Insert needle up between woven threads at A, using two strands of embroidery floss.
2. Loosely wrap floss once around needle.
3. Go down at B, the hole diagonally across from A. Pull floss taut as needle is pushed down through fabric.
4. Carry floss across back of work between knots.

Long Stitch

1. Insert needle up between woven threads at A.
2. Go down at B. Pull flat.

Repeat A–B for each stitch. Stitch may be horizontal, verticle, or diagonal as indicated in examples 1, 2, and 3. The length of the stitch should be the same as the length indicated on the graph.

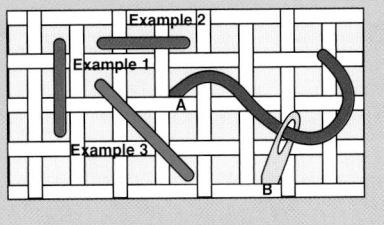

Continental Stitch

Stitches are done in a row working from right to left or top to bottom in vertical columns.

1. Insert needle up between woven threads at A.
2. Go down at B, the hole diagonally across from A.
3. Come back up at C and down at D, etc. The back side of stitching will result in long verticle stitches.

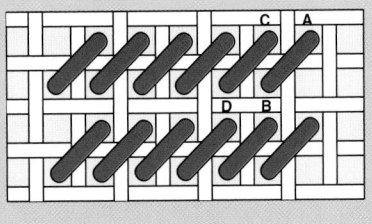

Bead Attachment

Beads should sit facing the same direction as the top cross-stitch.

1. Make first half of a cross-stitch.
2. Insert needle up between woven threads at A.
3. Pick up one bead before going down at B, the hole diagonally across from A.
4. To strengthen stitch, come up again at A and either go through bead again or split threads to lay around bead and go down at B again.

Wrapped Backstitch

1. Refer to Backstitch. Complete backstitches.
2. Insert needle up between woven threads at A.
3. Wrap over first stitch.
4. Go under second stitch. Be careful not to pierce the fabric or catch the backstitch.
5. Come up on the opposite side of the stitch at B. Continue the length of the backstitching. The effect can be varied by how loosely or tightly the floss is pulled when wrapping.

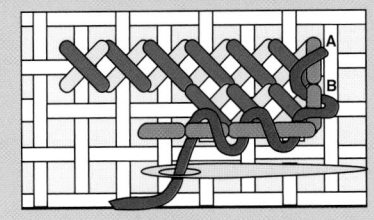

Satin Stitch

1. Insert needle up between woven threads at A.
2. Go down at B, forming a straight stitch.
3. Come up at C and go down at D, forming another smooth straight stitch that is slightly overlapping the first.
4. Repeat to fill design area.

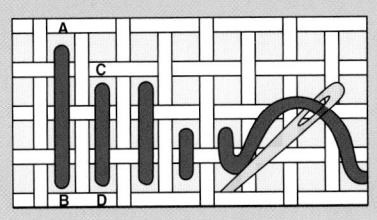

Cathedral Glass

The sample was stitched on Antique White Cashel Linen 28 over 2. The finished design size is 8⅝" x 17⅞". The fabric was cut 15" x 24".

Anchor DMC

Step 1: Cross-stitch (2 strands)

Anchor	DMC	
1		White
926		Ecru
386	746	Off White (1 strand)
300	745	Yellow–lt. pale (1 strand)
293	727	Topaz–vy. lt.
306	725	Topaz (1 strand)
307	783	Christmas Gold (1 strand)
891	676	Old Gold–lt.
890	729	Old Gold–med. (1 strand)
307	783	Christmas Gold (1 strand)
308	782	Topaz–med.
886	3047	Yellow Beige–lt.
881	945	Peach Beige
4146	950	Peach Pecan–dk. (1 strand)
882	3773	Pecan–vy. lt. (1 strand)
882	3773	Pecan–vy. lt.
892	225	Shell Pink– vy. lt.
969	3727	Antique Mauve–lt. (1 strand)
95	554	Violet–lt. (1 strand)
42	309	Rose–deep (1 strand)
98	553	Violet–med. (1 strand)
108	211	Lavender–lt. (1 strand)
869	3743	Antique Violet–vy. lt. (1 strand)
105	209	Lavender–dk.
110	208	Lavender–vy. dk. (1 strand)
101	327	Antique Violet–vy. dk. (1 strand)
870	3042	Antique Violet–lt.
117	3747	Blue Violet–lt.
121	794	Cornflower Blue–lt.
940	793	Cornflower Blue–med. (1 strand)
941	3807	Cornflower Blue (1 strand)
158	775	Baby Blue–vy. lt.
159	3325	Baby Blue–lt. (1 strand)
130	799	Delft–med. (1 strand)
130	799	Delft–med. (1 strand)
978	322	Navy Blue–vy. lt. (1 strand)
147	312	Navy Blue–lt.
160	3761	Sky Blue–lt.
264	772	Pine Green–lt. (1 strand)
265	3348	Yellow Green–lt. (1 strand)
266	3347	Yellow Green–med. (1 strand)
779	926	Slate Green (1 strand)
840	3768	Slate Green–dk. (1 strand)
851	924	Slate Green–vy. dk. (1 strand)
309	435	Brown–vy. lt. (1 strand)
379	840	Beige Brown–med. (1 strand)
887	372	Mustard–lt.
898	611	Drab Brown–dk.
905	3781	Mocha Brown–dk.
905	3781	Mocha Brown–dk. (1 strand)
382	3371	Black Brown (1 strand)
399	451	Shell Gray–dk.
399	451	Shell Gray–dk. (1 strand)
872	3740	Antique Violet–dk. (1 strand)
263	3799	Pewter Gray–vy. dk. (1 strand)
101	327	Antique Violet–vy. dk. (1 strand)
403	310	Black

Step 2: Backstitch (1 strand)

382	3371	Black Brown
403	310	Black

Step 3: French Knot (1 strand)

382	3371	Black Brown

Stitch Count: 120 width x 250 length

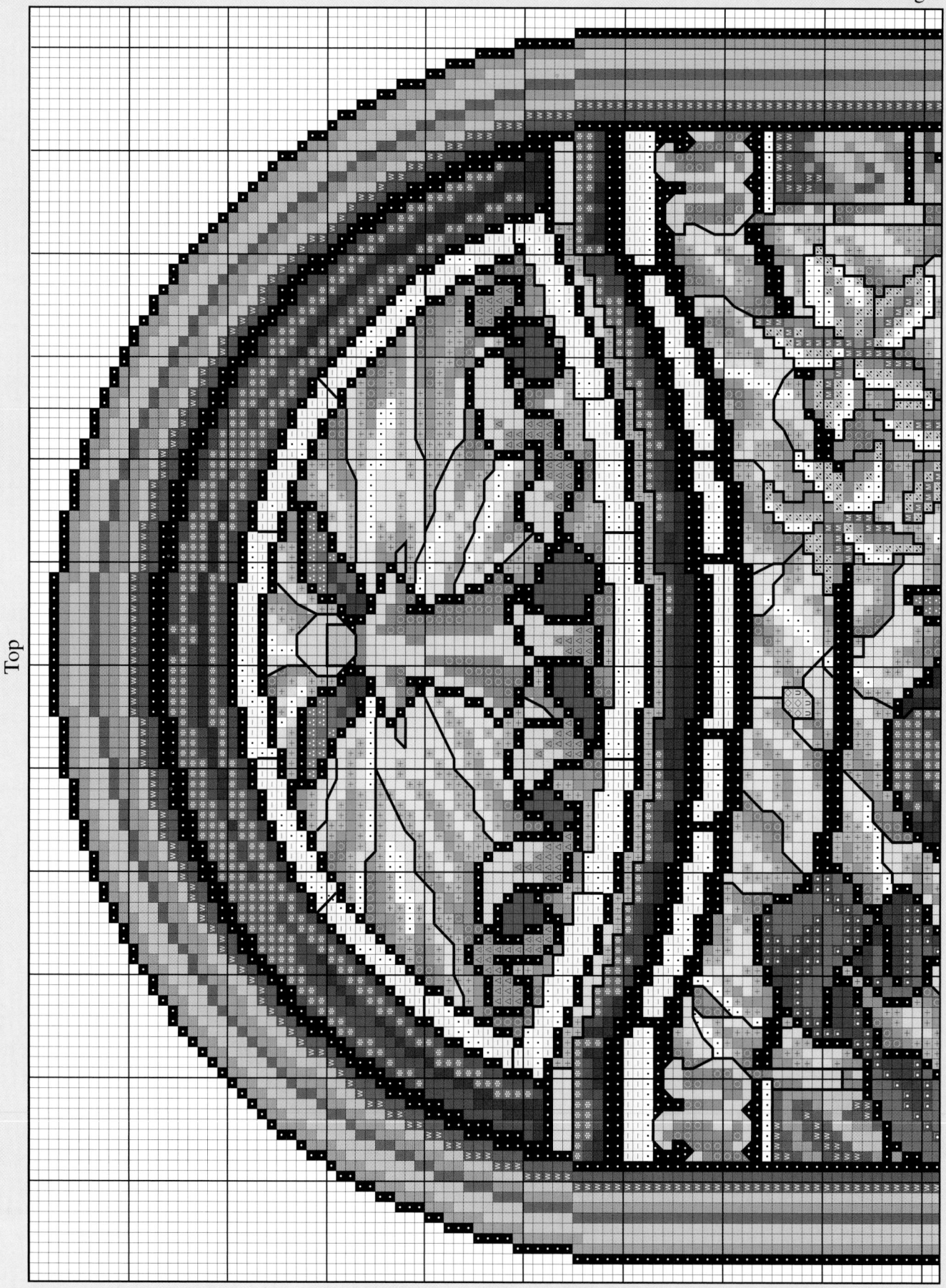

Top

Middle

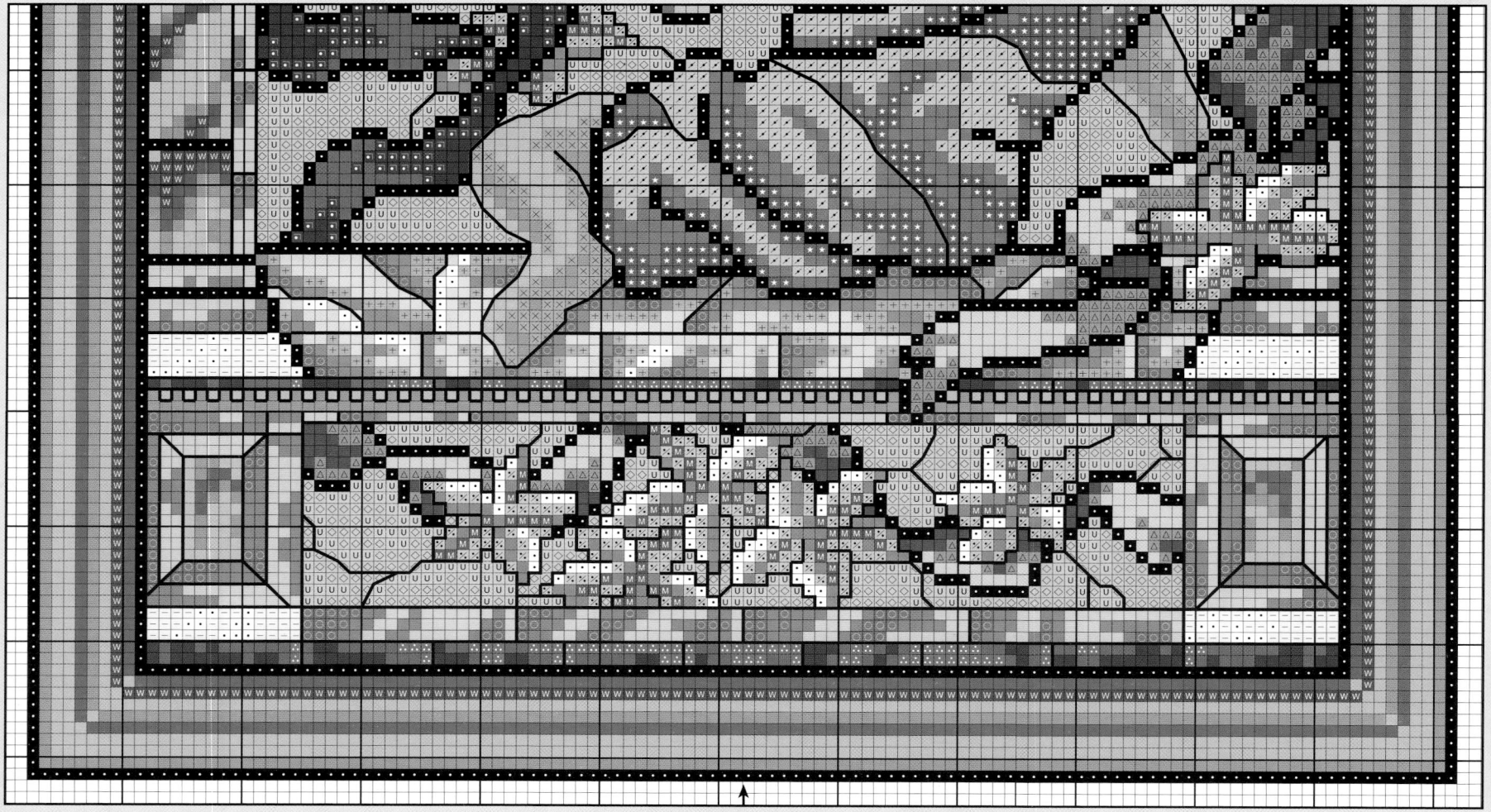

Bottom

Celestial Melody

The sample was stitched on Dirty Linen Cashel Linen 28 over 2. The finished design size is 6¾" x 6¾". The fabric was cut 13" x 13".

Anchor DMC

Step 1: Cross-stitch (2 strands)

Anchor	DMC	
1		White
300	745	Yellow–lt. pale
886	677	Old Gold–vy. lt.
886	677	Old Gold–vy. lt. (1 strand)
1		White (1 strand)
891	676	Old Gold–lt.
373	3045	Yellow Beige–dk.
10	352	Coral–lt.
8	761	Salmon–lt.
10	3712	Salmon–med.
897	221	Shell Pink–vy. dk.
5975	356	Terra Cotta–med.
5975	356	Terra Cotta–med. (1 strand)
5968	355	Terra Cotta–vy. dk. (1 strand)
1014	3830	Terra Cotta
160	813	Blue–lt.
920	932	Antique Blue–lt. (1 strand)
921	931	Antique Blue–med. (1 strand)
921	931	Antique Blue–med. (1 strand)
922	930	Antique Blue–dk. (1 strand)
849	927	Slate Green–med.
213	369	Pistachio Green–vy. lt. (1 strand)
265	3348	Yellow Green–lt. (1 strand)
861	3363	Pine Green–med.
860	3053	Green Gray
859	3052	Green Gray–med.
879	500	Blue Green–vy. dk. (1 strand)
861	3363	Pine Green–med. (1 strand)
868	758	Terra Cotta–lt. (1 strand)
933	3774	Peach Pecan–med. (1 strand)
868	758	Terra Cotta–lt. (1 strand)
860	3053	Green Gray (1 strand)
868	758	Terra Cotta–lt. (1 strand)
338	3776	Mahogany–lt. (1 strand)
914	3064	Pecan–lt.
933	3774	Peach Pecan–med.
933	3774	Peach Pecan–med. (1 strand)
1		White (1 strand)
914	3772	Pecan–med. (1 strand)
10	352	Coral–lt. (1 strand)
914	3772	Pecan–med. (1 strand)
5968	355	Terra Cotta–vy. dk. (1 strand)
914	3772	Pecan–med. (1 strand)
363	436	Tan (1 strand)
936	632	Pecan–dk.
388	3033	Mocha Brown–vy. lt.
956	613	Drab Brown–lt.
956	613	Drab Brown–lt. (1 strand)
8581	646	Beaver Gray–dk. (1 strand)
373	422	Hazel Nut Brown–lt.
889	370	Mustard–med.
889	370	Mustard–med. (1 strand)
921	931	Antique Blue–med. (1 strand)
347	402	Mahogany–vy. lt.
347	402	Mahogany–vy. lt. (1 strand)
886	677	Old Gold–vy. lt. (1 strand)
338	3776	Mahogany–lt.
942	738	Tan–vy. lt.
363	436	Tan
363	436	Tan (1 strand)
891	676	Old Gold–lt. (1 strand)
379	840	Beige Brown–med.
381	838	Beige Brown–vy. dk. (1 strand)
936	632	Pecan–dk. (1 strand)
8581	646	Beaver Gray–dk.
273	3787	Brown Gray–dk. (1 strand)
846	3051	Green Gray–dk. (1 strand)
401	844	Beaver Gray–ultra dk.
397	762	Pearl Gray–vy. lt.
397	762	Pearl Gray–vy. lt. (1 strand)
343	3752	Antique Blue–vy. lt. (1 strand)
403	310	Black (1 strand)
879	500	Blue Green–vy. dk. (1 strand)
403	310	Black

Step 2: Backstitch (1 strand)

Anchor	DMC	
381	838	Beige Brown–vy. dk.

Step 3: Long Stitch (1 strand)

Anchor	DMC	
936	632	Pecan–dk.

Stitch Count: 95 width x 95 length

Angels

Cherubic Garden

The sample was stitched on Antique White Cashel Linen 28 over 2. The finished design size is 14" x 11". The fabric was cut 20" x 17".

Anchor DMC

Step 1: Cross-stitch (2 strands)

Anchor	DMC	
300	3823	Yellow–ultra pale
300	3823	Yellow–ultra pale (1 strand)
891	676	Old Gold–lt. (1 strand)
300	3823	Yellow–ultra pale (1 strand)
301	744	Yellow–pale (1 strand)
301	744	Yellow–pale (1 strand)
297	743	Yellow–med. (1 strand)
891	676	Old Gold–lt.
297	743	Yellow–med. (1 strand)
890	729	Old Gold–med. (1 strand)
891	676	Old Gold–lt. (1 strand)
118	340	Blue Violet–med. (1 strand)
890	729	Old Gold–med. (1 strand)
118	340	Blue Violet–med. (1 strand)
881	945	Peach Beige
881	945	Peach Beige (1 strand)
363	436	Tan (1 strand)
10	352	Coral–lt.
11	351	Coral
1014	3830	Terra Cotta
50	605	Cranberry–vy. lt.
50	605	Cranberry–vy. lt. (1 strand)
76	603	Cranberry (1 strand)
76	603	Cranberry (1 strand)
87	3607	Plum–lt. (1 strand)
87	3607	Plum–lt. (1 strand)
78	3803	Mauve–dk. (1 strand)
117	3747	Blue Violet–vy. lt. (1 strand)
1		White (1 strand)
117	3747	Blue Violet–vy. lt. (1 strand)
118	340	Blue Violet–med. (1 strand)
118	340	Blue Violet–med. (1 strand)
119	3746	Blue Violet–dk. (1 strand)
119	3746	Blue Violet–dk. (1 strand)
101	327	Antique Violet–vy. dk. (1 strand)
101	327	Antique Violet–vy. dk. (1 strand)
944	869	Hazel Nut Brown–vy. dk. (1 strand)
158	3756	Baby Blue–ultra vy. lt.
158	3756	Baby Blue–ultra vy. lt. (1 strand)
343	3752	Antique Blue–vy. lt. (1 strand)
343	3752	Antique Blue–vy. lt.
343	3752	Antique Blue–vy. lt. (1 strand)
160	813	Blue–lt. (1 strand)
264	472	Avocado Green–ultra lt.
264	472	Avocado Green–ultra lt. (1 strand)
266	581	Moss Green (1 strand)
257	3346	Hunter Green
257	3346	Hunter Green (1 strand)
879	500	Blue Green–vy. dk. (1 strand)
279	734	Olive Green–lt.
280	733	Olive Green–med.
889	831	Olive Green
843	3364	Pine Green
861	3363	Pine Green–med.
861	3363	Pine Green–med. (1 strand)
879	500	Blue Green–vy. dk. (1 strand)
363	436	Tan
363	436	Tan (1 strand)
944	869	Hazel Nut Brown–vy. dk. (1 strand)

Step 2: Backstitch (1 strand)

Anchor	DMC	
78	3803	Mauve–dk. (2 strands) (Lettering)
78	3803	Mauve–dk.
257	3346	Hunter Green
879	500	Blue Green–vy. dk.
944	869	Hazel Nut Brown–vy. dk.
381	938	Coffee Brown–ultra dk.

Step 3: Long Stitch (2 strands)

Anchor	DMC	
1		White
264	472	Avocado Green–ultra lt.

Stitch Count: 196 width x 154 length

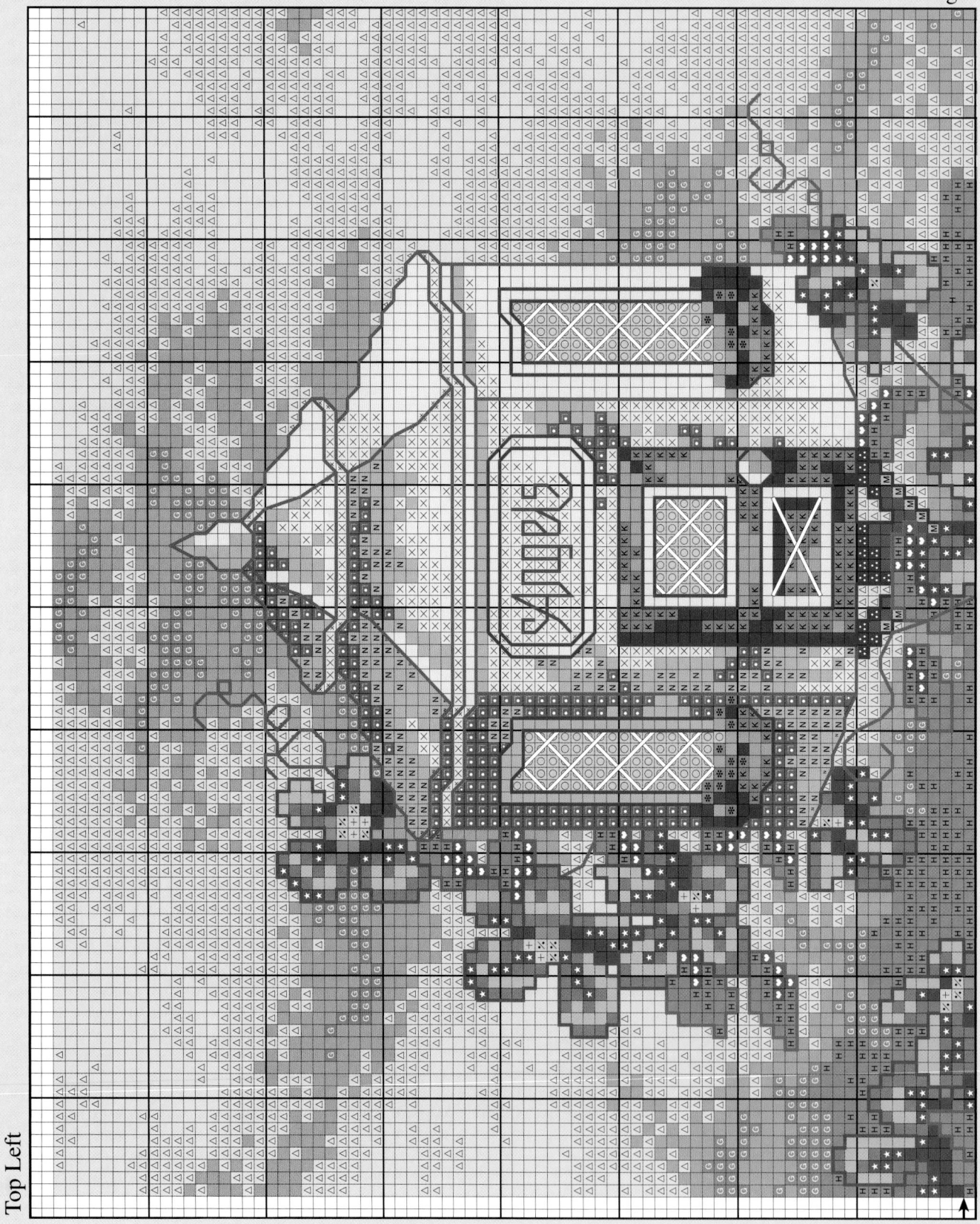

Top Left

Top Right

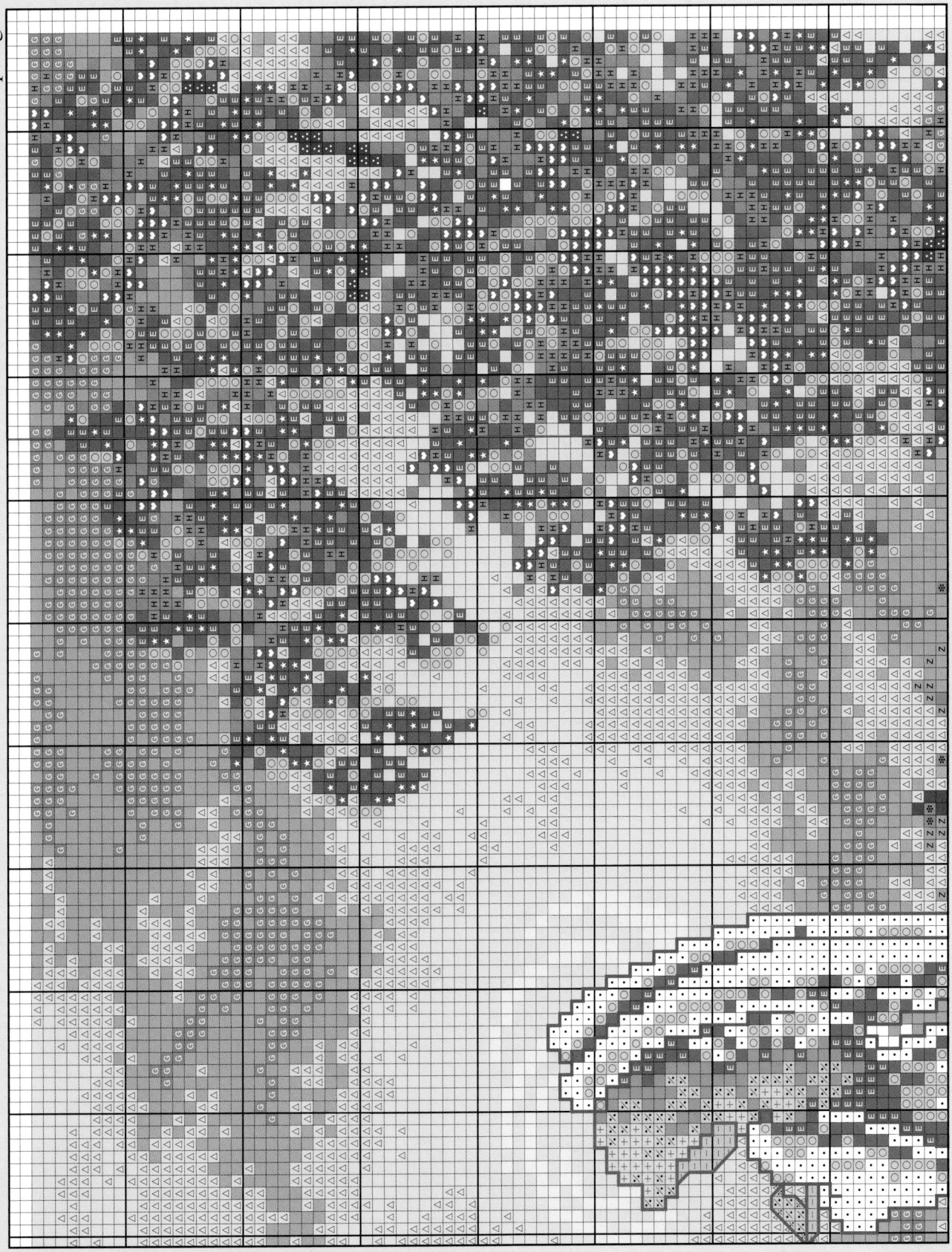

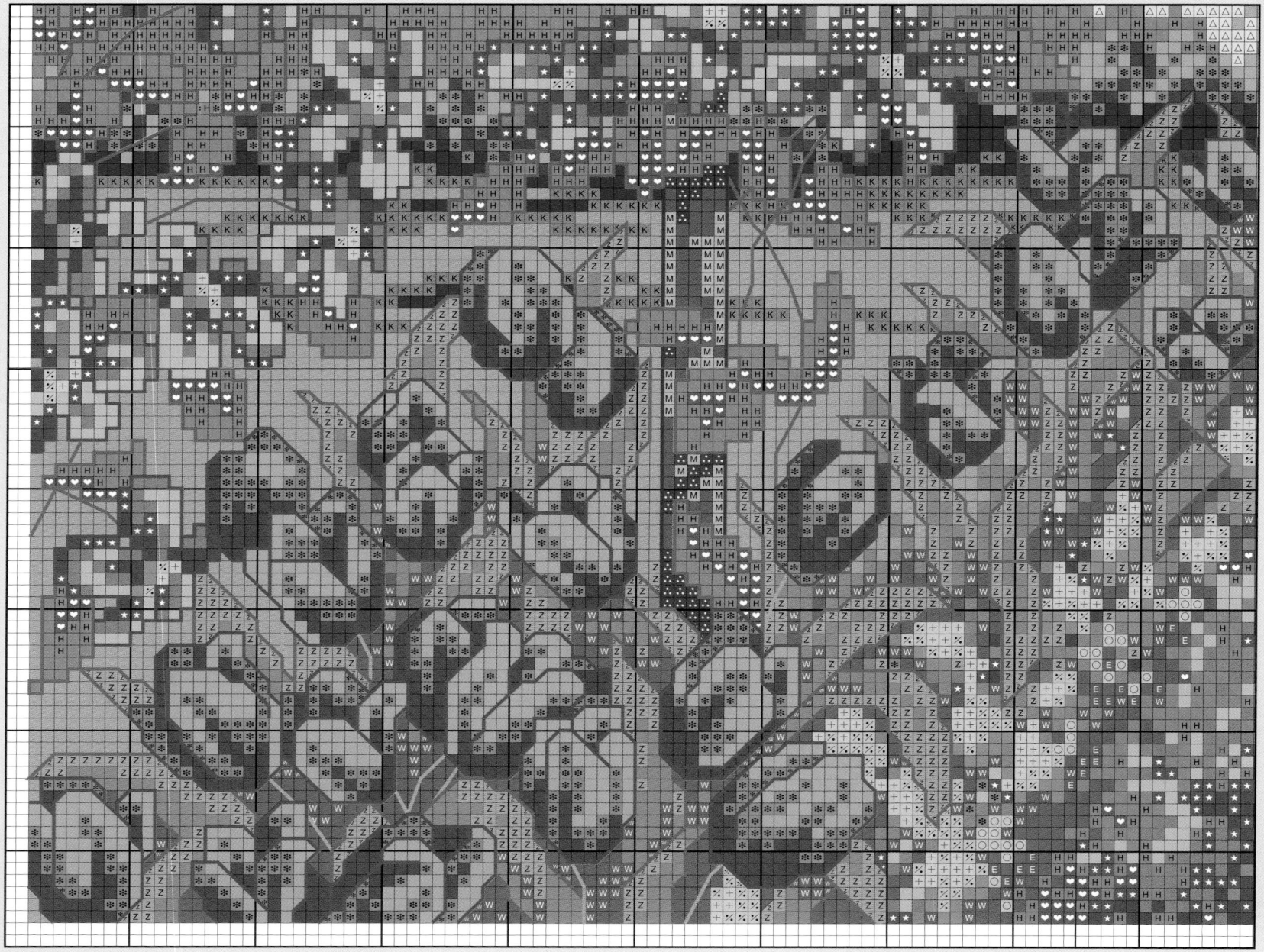

Bottom Left

Bottom Right

The Road to Bethlehem

The sample was stitched on Vintage Linen 28 over 2. The finished design size is 6⅛" x 4⅝". The fabric was cut 13" x 11".

Anchor	DMC	
Step 1:	**Cross-stitch (2 strands)**	
387	712	Cream
886	677	Old Gold–vy. lt.
887	3046	Yellow Beige–med.
301	744	Yellow–pale
307	783	Christmas Gold
881	945	Peach Beige
86	3608	Plum–vy. lt.
87	3607	Plum–lt.
78	3803	Mauve–dk.
104	210	Lavender–med. (1 strand)
118	340	Blue Violet–med. (1 strand)
118	340	Blue Violet–med.
158	775	Baby Blue–vy. lt.
159	827	Blue–vy. lt.
121	793	Cornflower Blue–med.
940	792	Cornflower Blue–dk.
779	926	Slate Green
779	926	Slate Green (1 strand)
922	930	Antique Blue–dk. (1 strand)
213	504	Blue Green–lt.
264	472	Avocado Green–ultra lt.
844	3012	Khaki Green–med.
844	3012	Khaki Green–med. (1 strand)
846	3051	Green Gray–dk. (1 strand)
363	436	Tan
832	612	Drab Brown–med.
830	644	Beige Gray–med.
392	642	Beige Gray–dk.
903	640	Beige Gray–vy. dk. (1 strand)
382	3021	Brown Gray–vy. dk. (1 strand)
382	3021	Brown Gray–vy. dk. (1 strand)
236	3799	Pewter Gray–vy. dk. (1 strand)
Step 2:	**Continental Stitch (2 strands)**	
301	744	Yellow–pale
104	210	Lavender–med. (1 strand)
118	340	Blue Violet–med. (1 strand)
846	3051	Green Gray–dk.
373	422	Hazel Nut Brown–lt.
307	977	Golden Brown–lt.
382	3021	Brown Gray–vy. dk.
Step 3:	**Backstitch (1 strand)**	
307	783	Christmas Gold (2 strands)
872	3740	Antique Violet–dk.
382	3021	Brown Gray–vy. dk.
Step 4:	**Long Stitch (2 strands)**	
387	712	Cream

Stitch Count: 85 width x 64 length

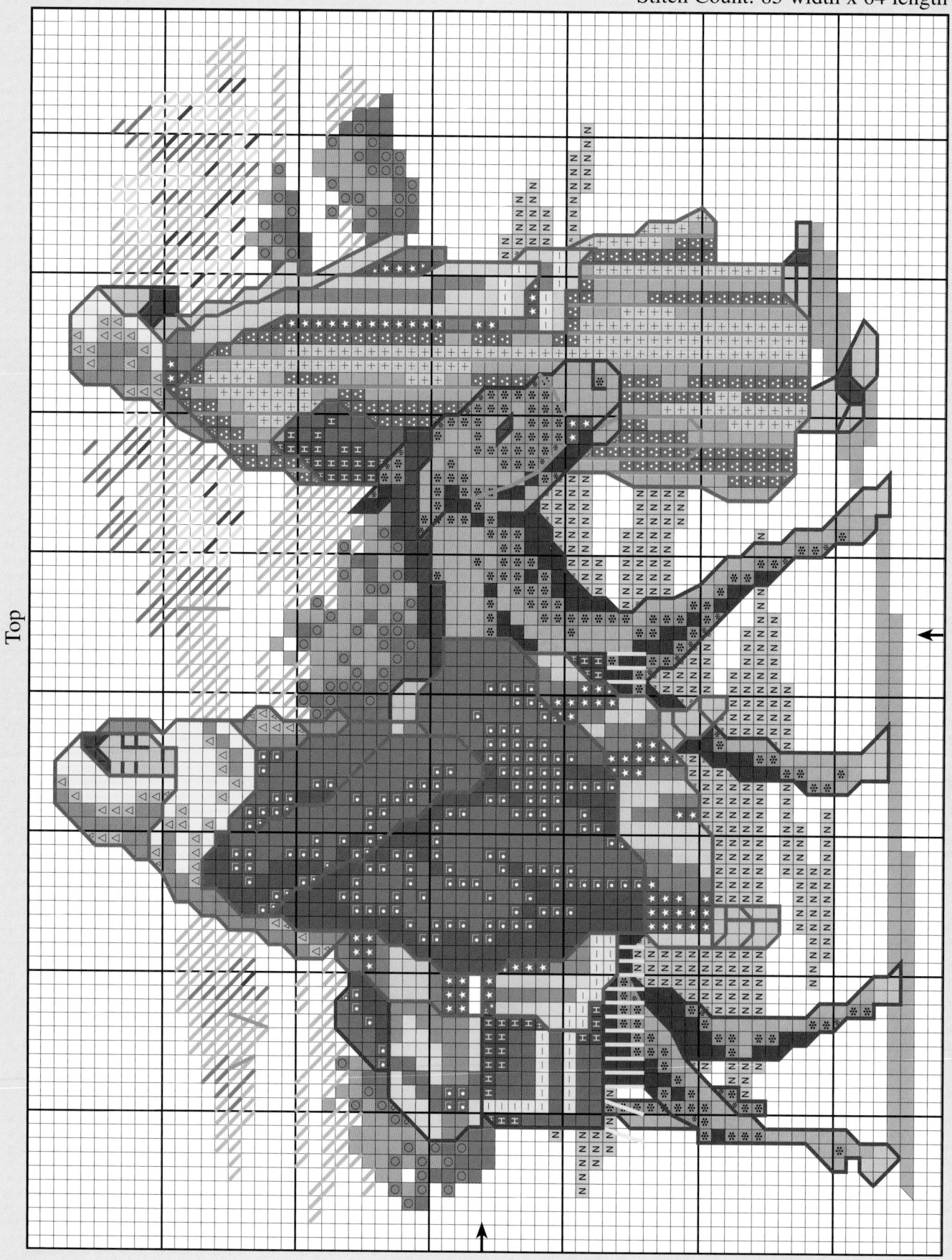

Nations shall come to your light
And kings to the brightness of your rising
Isaiah 60:3

Three Wise Men

The sample was stitched on Smokey Pearl Cashel Linen 28 over 2. The finished design size is 5⅜" x 7⅞". The fabric was cut 12" x 14".

Anchor	DMC	
Step 1:	**Cross-stitch (2 strands)**	
387	712	Cream
300	3823	Yellow–ultra pale
305	3822	Straw–lt.
301	744	Yellow–pale
4146	754	Peach–lt.
50	3716	Wild Rose–lt.
69	3687	Mauve
78	3803	Mauve–dk.
86	3608	Plum–vy. lt.
87	3607	Plum–lt. (1 strand)
105	209	Lavender–dk. (1 strand)
88	718	Plum (1 strand)
99	552	Violet–dk. (1 strand)
872	3740	Antique Violet–dk.
928	3811	Turquoise–vy. lt.
168	807	Peacock Blue
168	807	Peacock Blue (1 strand)
1066	3809	Turquoise–vy. dk. (1 strand)
1066	3809	Turquoise–vy. dk. (1 strand)
149	311	Navy Blue–med.(1 strand)
130	799	Delft–med.
978	322	Navy Blue–vy. lt.
162	824	Blue–dk.
842	3013	Khaki Green–lt.
844	3012	Khaki Green–med. (1 strand)
870	3042	Antique Violet–lt. (1 strand)
874	833	Olive Green–lt.
874	833	Olive Green–lt. (1 strand)
871	3041	Antique Violet–med. (1 strand)
362	437	Tan–lt.
362	437	Tan–lt. (1 strand)
375	420	Hazel Nut Brown–dk. (1 strand)
375	420	Hazel Nut Brown–dk. (1 strand)
380	839	Beige Brown–dk. (1 strand)
830	644	Beige Gray–med.
392	642	Beige Gray–dk.
8581	646	Beaver Gray–dk.
273	3787	Brown Gray–dk.
Step 2:	**Backstitch (1 strand)**	
872	3740	Antique Violet–dk.
149	311	Navy Blue–med.
874	833	Olive Green–lt. (2 strands)
375	420	Hazel Nut Brown–dk.
380	839	Beige Brown–dk.
273	3787	Brown Gray–dk.
Step 3:	**French Knot (1 strand)**	
872	3740	Antique Violet–dk.
149	311	Navy Blue–med.

Stitch Count: 75 width x 110 length

Mary & the Christ Child

The sample was stitched on Platinum Dublin Linen 25 over 2. The finished design size is 9¼" x 12⅝". The fabric was cut 16" x 19".

Anchor DMC

Step 1: Cross-stitch (2 strands)

Anchor	DMC	Color
1		White
386	3823	Yellow–ultra pale
300	745	Yellow–lt. pale
891	676	Old Gold–lt.
891	676	Old Gold–lt. (1 strand)
386	3823	Yellow–ultra pale (1 strand)
366	951	Peach Pecan–lt.
881	945	Peach Beige
881	945	Peach Beige (1 strand)
868	758	Terra Cotta–lt. (1 strand)
48	818	Baby Pink
8	761	Salmon–lt.
9	760	Salmon
892	225	Shell Pink–vy. lt.
893	224	Shell Pink–lt.
893	224	Shell Pink–lt. (1 strand)
894	223	Shell Pink–med. (1 strand)
896	3722	Shell Pink
896	3722	Shell Pink (1 strand)
9	760	Salmon (1 strand)
108	211	Lavender–lt.
108	211	Lavender–lt. (1 strand)
105	209	Lavender–dk. (1 strand)
105	209	Lavender–dk.
105	209	Lavender–dk. (1 strand)
871	3041	Antique Violet–med. (1 strand)
870	3042	Antique Violet–lt.
871	3041	Antique Violet–med.
870	3042	Antique Violet–lt. (1 strand)
117	3747	Blue Violet–vy. lt. (1 strand)
117	3747	Blue Violet–vy. lt. (1 strand)
1		White (1 strand)
347	402	Mahogany–vy. lt.
338	3776	Mahogany–lt.
387	822	Beige Gray–lt.
874	834	Olive Green–vy. lt.
944	869	Hazel Nut Brown–vy. dk.
956	613	Drab Brown–lt. (1 strand)
387	822	Beige Gray–lt. (1 strand)
956	613	Drab Brown–lt.
898	611	Drab Brown–dk. (1 strand)
891	676	Old Gold–lt. (1 strand)

Step 2: Backstitch (1 strand)

Anchor	DMC	Color
896	3722	Shell Pink
1019	3802	Antique Mauve–deep
871	3041	Antique Violet–med.
874	834	Olive Green–vy. lt.
944	869	Hazel Nut Brown–vy. dk.
956	613	Drab Brown–lt. (2 strands)
898	611	Drab Brown–dk.

Glory to God in the highest, and on earth peace, good will toward men. -- Luke 2:14

Stitch Count: 116 width x 158 length

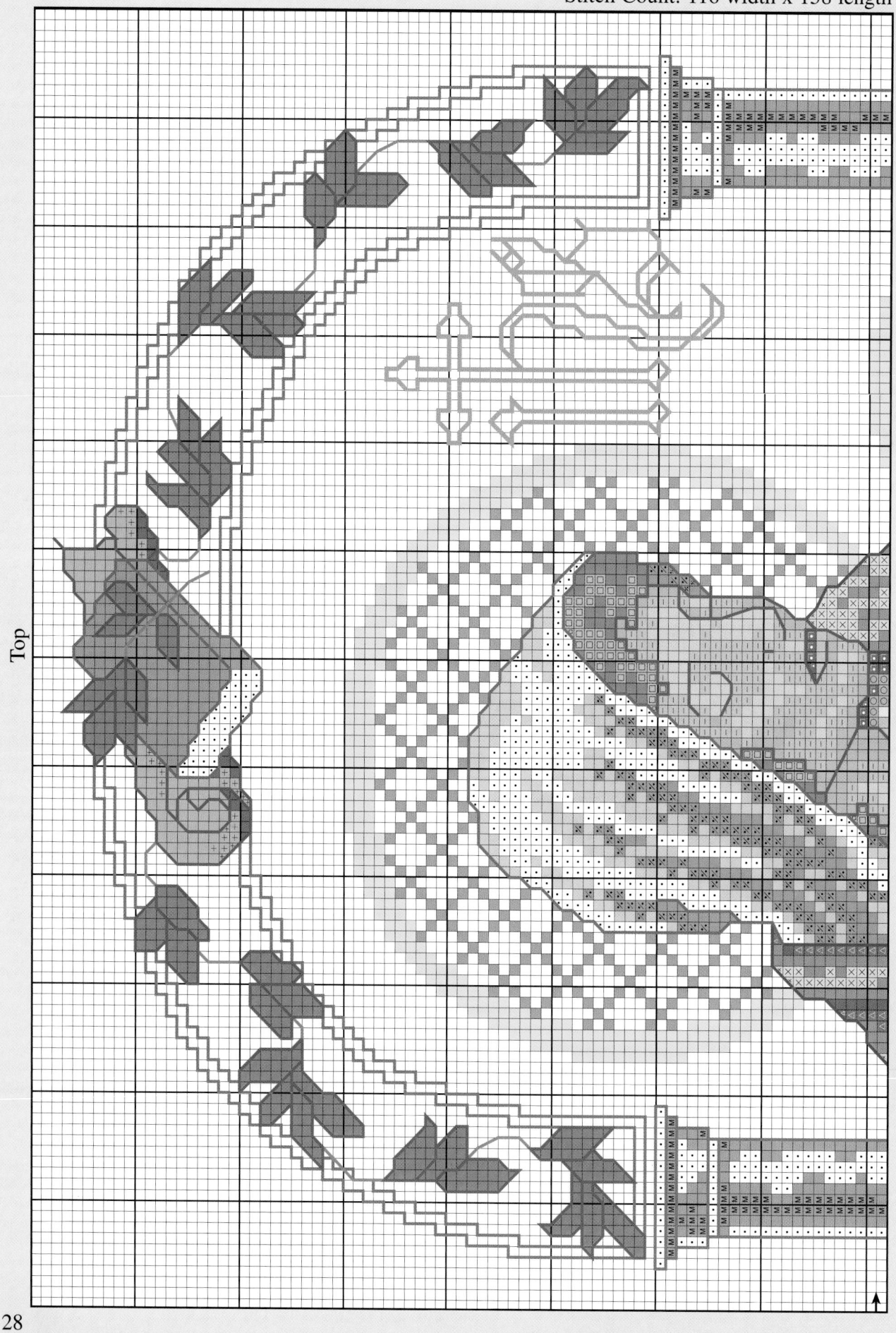

Top

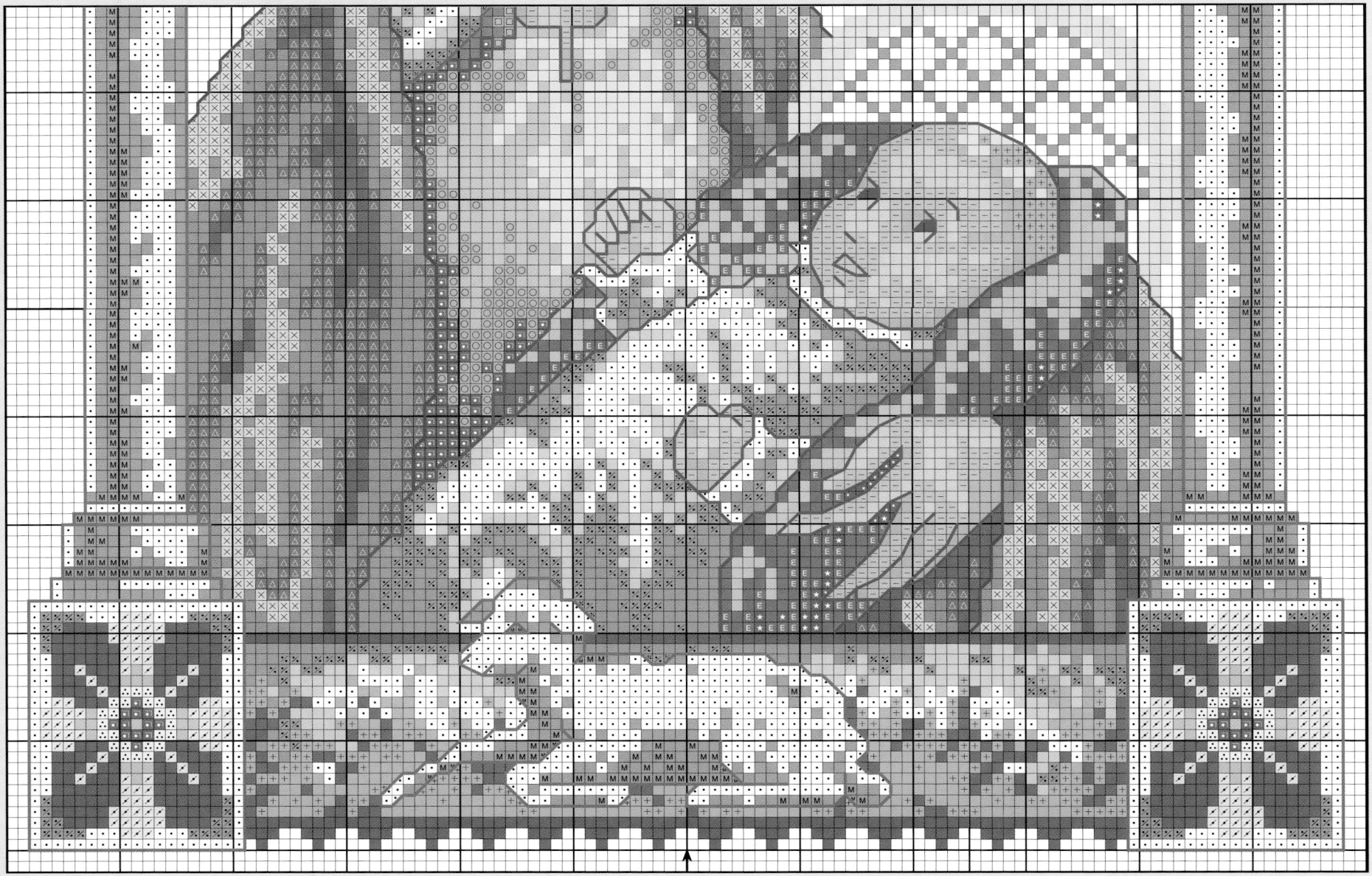

Bottom

Jesus & the Children

The sample was stitched on Antique White Cashel Linen 28 over 2. The finished design size is 7⅞" x 13⅝". The fabric was cut 14" x 20".

Anchor DMC

Step 1: Cross-stitch (2 strands)

Anchor	DMC	
1		White
886	677	Old Gold–vy. lt.
891	676	Old Gold–lt.
366	951	Peach Pecan–lt.
4146	950	Peach Pecan–dk.
4146	950	Peach Pecan–dk. (1 strand)
882	3773	Pecan–vy. lt. (1 strand)
50	3716	Wild Rose–lt. (1 strand)
969	3727	Antique Mauve–lt. (1 strand)
75	3733	Dusty Rose–lt. (1 strand)
969	316	Antique Mauve–med. (1 strand)
69	3687	Mauve (1 strand)
970	3726	Antique Mauve–dk. (1 strand)
968	778	Antique Mauve–vy. lt.
969	3727	Antique Mauve–lt.
969	316	Antique Mauve–med.
969	316	Antique Mauve–med. (1 strand)
970	3726	Antique Mauve–dk. (1 strand)
970	3726	Antique Mauve–dk.
970	315	Antique Mauve–vy. dk.
869	3743	Antique Violet–vy. lt.
869	3743	Antique Violet–vy. lt. (1 strand)
117	3747	Blue Violet–vy. lt. (1 strand)
870	3042	Antique Violet–lt. (1 strand)
117	341	Blue Violet–lt. (1 strand)
871	3041	Antique Violet–med. (1 strand)
118	340	Blue Violet–med. (1 strand)
876	3740	Antique Violet–dk. (1 strand)
119	3746	Blue Violet–dk. (1 strand)
117	3747	Blue Violet–vy. lt.
117	3747	Blue Violet–vy. lt. (1 strand)
117	341	Blue Violet–lt. (1 strand)
117	341	Blue Violet–lt.
121	794	Cornflower Blue–dk.
121	793	Cornflower Blue–med.
121	793	Cornflower Blue–med. (1 strand)
940	792	Cornflower Blue–dk. (1 strand)
940	792	Cornflower Blue–dk. (1 strand)
876	3740	Antique Violet–dk. (1 strand)
858	524	Fern Green–vy. lt. (1 strand)
213	504	Blue Green–lt.(1 strand)
859	523	Fern Green–lt. (1 strand)
875	503	Blue Green–med. (1 strand)
859	522	Fern Green (1 strand)
876	502	Blue Green (1 strand)
875	503	Blue Green–med.
876	502	Blue Green
878	501	Blue Green–dk.
878	501	Blue Green–dk. (1 strand)
840	3768	Slate Green–dk. (1 strand)
879	500	Blue Green–vy. dk.
347	402	Mahogany–vy. lt.
338	3776	Mahogany–lt.
349	301	Mahogany–med.
888	3828	Hazel Nut Brown
885	739	Tan–ultra vy. lt.
362	437	Tan–lt.
379	840	Beige Brown–med.
380	839	Beige Brown–dk.
397	762	Pearl Gray–vy. lt. (1 strand)
869	3743	Antique Violet–vy. lt. (1 strand)
397	762	Pearl Gray–vy. lt. (1 strand)
213	504	Blue Green–lt. (1 strand)
398	415	Pearl Gray (1 strand)
849	927	Slate Green–med. (1 strand)
398	415	Pearl Gray (1 strand)
875	503	Blue Green–med. (1 strand)
399	318	Steel Gray–lt. (1 strand)
121	793	Cornflower Blue–med. (1 strand)
399	318	Steel Gray–lt. (1 strand)
849	927	Slate Green–med. (1 strand)
399	318	Steel Gray–lt. (1 strand)
876	502	Blue Green (1 strand)

Step 2: Backstitch (1 strand)

Anchor	DMC	
970	315	Antique Mauve–vy. dk.
871	3041	Antique Violet–med.
876	3740	Antique Violet–dk.
840	3768	Slate Green–dk.
379	840	Beige Brown–med.

Stitch Count: 111 width x 191 length

380 839 Beige Brown–dk.

Step 3: French Knot (1 strand)

969 3727 Antique Mauve–lt.

Step 4: Long Stitch (1 strand)

379 840 Beige Brown–med.

Step 5: Beadwork

02001 Pearl

Bottom

CHRIST IS BORN
NUELULIX
NUELULIX

Scenes of the Nativity

The samples were stitched on Vintage Linen 32 over 2. The finished design size for the left and right sections is 4¾" x 9½". The finished design size for the middle section is 6¼" x 12½". The fabric for the left and right sections was cut 11" x 17". The fabric for the middle section was cut 13" x 19".

Anchor DMC

Step 1: Cross-stitch (2 strands)

Anchor	DMC	
387	712	Cream
387	712	Cream (1 strand)
956	613	Drab Brown–lt. (1 strand)
300	745	Yellow–lt. pale
300	745	Yellow–lt. pale (1 strand)
886	677	Old Gold–vy. lt. (1 strand)
886	677	Old Gold–vy. lt.
891	676	Old Gold–lt.
891	676	Old Gold–lt. (1 strand)
306	725	Topaz (1 strand)
891	676	Old Gold–lt. (1 strand)
307	783	Christmas Gold (1 strand)
307	783	Christmas Gold
305	3822	Straw–lt.
306	3820	Straw–dk.
373	3045	Yellow Beige–dk.
881	945	Peach Beige
868	3779	Terra Cotta–vy. lt.
868	3779	Terra Cotta–vy. lt. (1 strand)
9	760	Salmon (1 strand)
271	3713	Salmon–vy. lt.
9	760	Salmon (1 strand)
896	3722	Shell Pink (1 strand)
11	3328	Salmon–dk. (1 strand)
897	221	Shell Pink–vy. dk. (1 strand)
74	3354	Dusty Rose–vy. lt.
969	316	Antique Mauve–med.
970	3726	Antique Mauve–dk.
117	3747	Blue Violet–vy. lt.
117	341	Blue Violet–lt.
121	793	Cornflower Blue–med.
940	3807	Cornflower Blue (1 strand)
940	792	Cornflower Blue–dk. (1 strand)
130	799	Delft–med. (1 strand)
131	798	Delft–dk. (1 strand)
132	797	Royal Blue
150	823	Navy Blue–dk.
214	966	Baby Green–med.
216	367	Pistachio Green–dk.
265	3348	Yellow Green–lt. (1 strand)
860	3053	Green Gray (1 strand)
843	3364	Pine Green
861	3363	Pine Green–med.
861	3363	Pine Green–med. (1 strand)
862	520	Fern Green–dk. (1 strand)
876	3816	Celadon Green
877	3815	Celadon Green–dk.
879	500	Blue Green–vy. dk.
851	924	Slate Green–vy. dk.
942	738	Tan–vy. lt.
362	437	Tan–lt. (1 strand)
886	677	Old Gold–vy. lt. (1 strand)
362	437	Tan–lt. (1 strand)
888	3828	Hazel Nut Brown (1 strand)
363	436	Tan
832	612	Drab Brown–med.
888	3828	Hazel Nut Brown (1 strand)
375	420	Hazel Nut Brown–dk. (1 strand)
375	420	Hazel Nut Brown–dk. (1 strand)
380	839	Beige Brown–dk. (1 strand)
8581	3023	Brown Gray–lt.
8581	3022	Brown Gray–med.
382	3021	Brown Gray–vy. dk.
905	645	Beaver Gray–vy. dk.
403	310	Black

Step 2: Backstitch (1 strand)

Anchor	DMC	
387	712	Cream (2 strands)
305	3822	Straw–lt.
306	3820	Straw–dk.
306	3820	Straw–dk. (2 strands) (halo)
881	945	Peach Beige (2 strands)
896	3722	Shell Pink
11	3328	Salmon–dk.
74	3354	Dusty Rose–vy. lt.

Stitch Count: 100 width x 201 length

Top of **Middle Section**

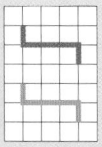

970 3726 Antique Mauve–dk.

264 472 Avocado Green–ultra lt. (2 strands)

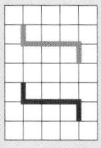

832 612 Drab Brown–med.

382 3021 Brown Gray–vy. dk.

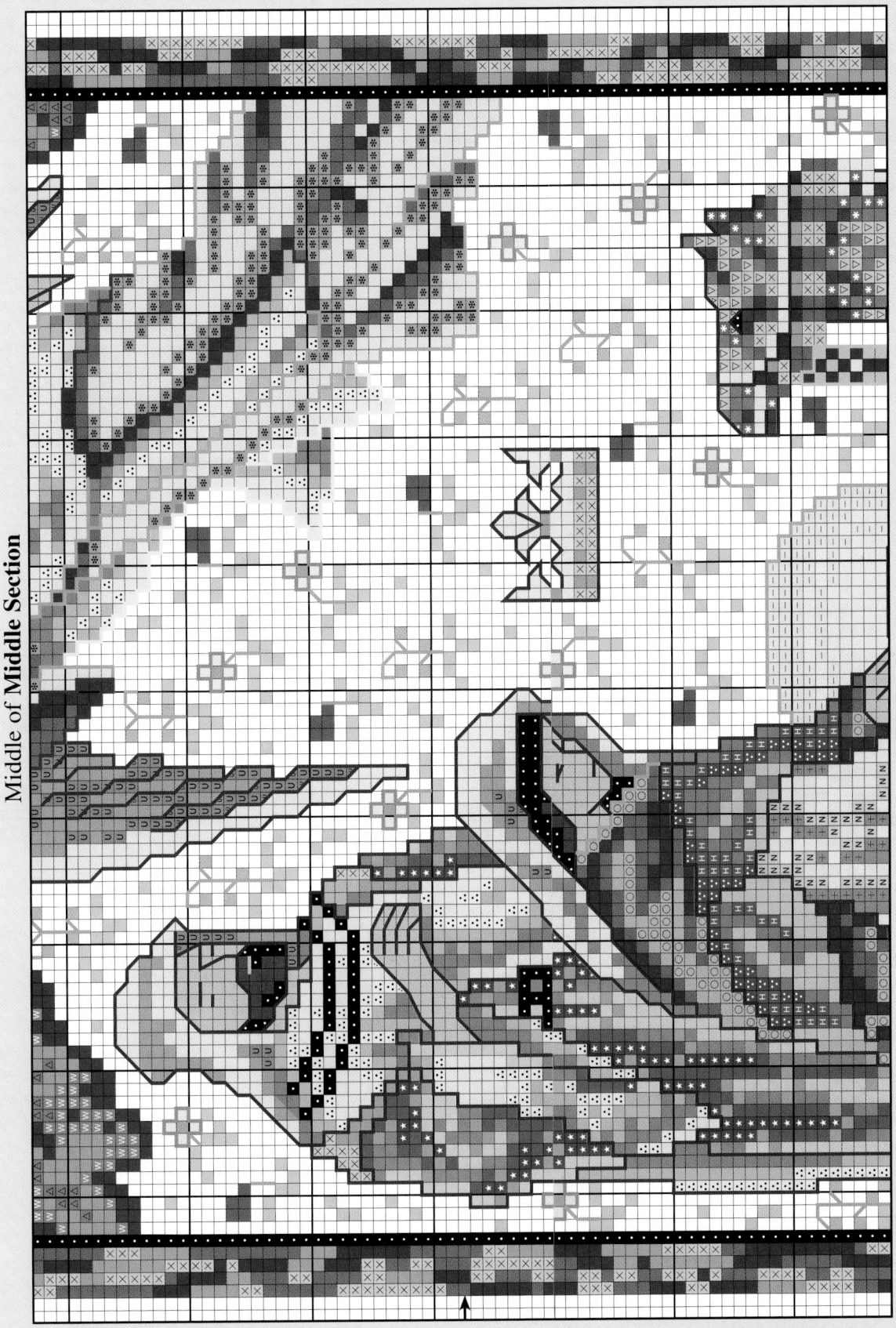

382 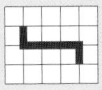 3021 Brown Gray–vy. dk. (2 strands) (eyes)

Step 3: French Knot (1 strand)

11 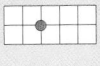 3328 Salmon–dk.

Bottom of **Middle Section**

Top of **Left Section** Stitch Count: 75 width x 151 length

Stitch Count: 75 width x 151 length

Top of **Right Section**

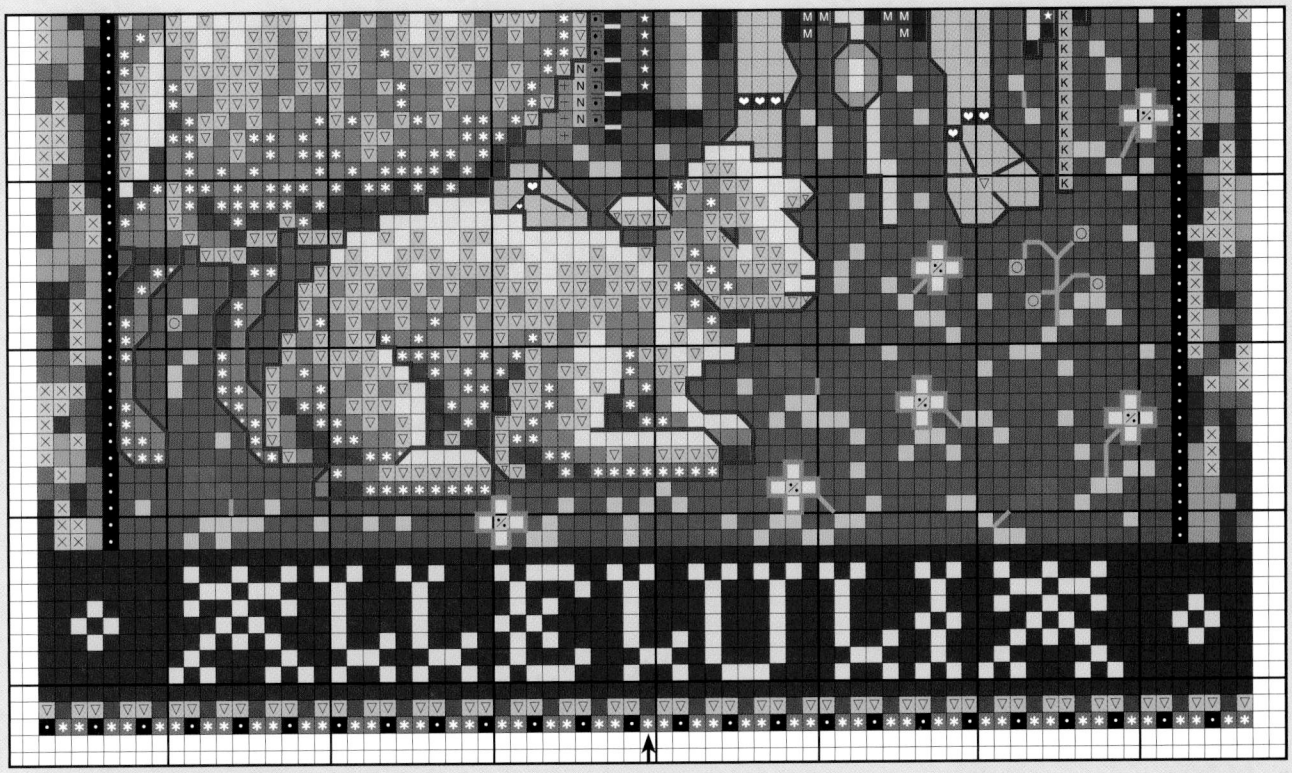

Bottom of **Left Section**

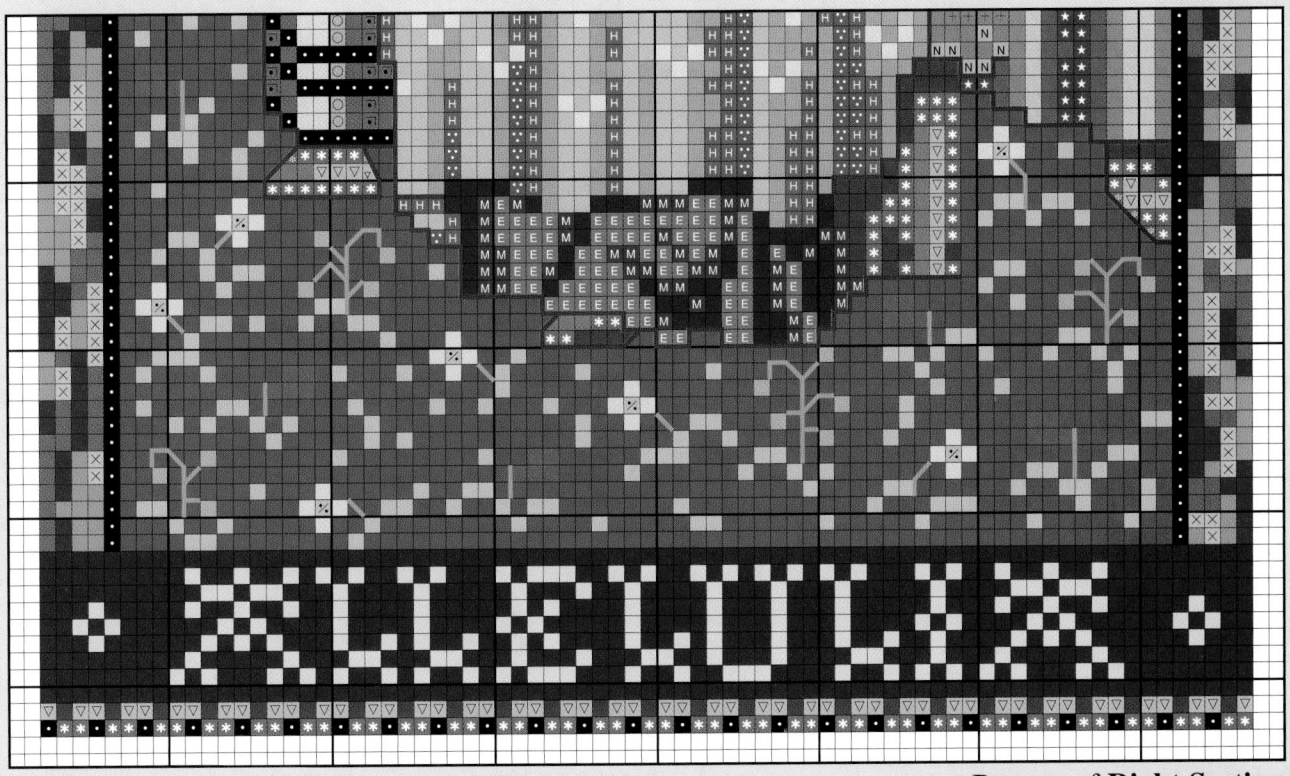

Bottom of **Right Section**

Last Supper

The sample was stitched on Light Mocha Cashel Linen 28 over 2. The finished design size is 17⅞" x 11⅝". The fabric was cut 24" x 18".

Anchor	DMC	

Step 1: Cross-stitch (2 strands)

Anchor	DMC	
387	712	Cream
387	712	Cream (1 strand)
891	676	Old Gold–lt. (1 strand)
387	712	Cream (1 strand)
942	738	Tan– vy. lt. (1 strand)
891	676	Old Gold–lt.
886	3047	Yellow Beige–lt.
887	3046	Yellow Beige–med.
373	3045	Yellow Beige–dk.
881	945	Peach Beige (1 strand)
882	3773	Pecan–vy. lt. (1 strand)
882	3773	Pecan–vy. lt.
892	819	Baby Pink–lt.
892	819	Baby Pink–lt. (1 strand)
25	3326	Rose–lt. (1 strand)
50	605	Cranberry–vy. lt.
50	605	Cranberry–vy. lt. (1 strand)
76	961	Wild Rose–dk. (1 strand)
25	3326	Rose–lt.
25	3326	Rose–lt. (1 strand)
894	223	Shell Pink–med. (1 strand)
76	961	Wild Rose–dk.
42	3350	Dusty Rose–dk.
894	223	Shell Pink–med.
896	3722	Shell Pink
78	3803	Mauve–dk.
1019	3802	Antique Mauve–deep
99	552	Violet–dk.
99	552	Violet–dk. (1 strand)
101	550	Violet–vy. dk. (1 strand)
101	550	Violet–vy.dk.
872	3740	Antique Violet–dk.
872	3740	Antique Violet–dk. (1 strand)
119	333	Blue Violet–vy. dk. (1 strand)
117	341	Blue Violet–lt.
118	340	Blue Violet–med.
118	340	Blue Violet–med. (1 strand)
119	333	Blue Violet–vy. dk. (1 strand)
130	809	Delft
130	799	Delft–med.
131	798	Delft–dk.
132	797	Royal Blue
134	820	Royal Blue–vy. dk.
121	793	Cornflower Blue–med.
940	792	Cornflower Blue–dk.
940	792	Cornflower Blue–dk. (1 strand)
941	791	Cornflower Blue–vy. dk. (1 strand)
941	791	Cornflower Blue–vy. dk.
941	791	Cornflower Blue–vy. dk. (1 strand)
845	3011	Khaki Green–dk. (1 strand)
842	3013	Khaki Green–lt.
844	3012	Khaki Green–med.
845	3011	Khaki Green–dk.
874	834	Olive Green–vy. lt.
874	833	Olive Green–lt.
889	831	Olive Green–med.
942	738	Tan–vy. lt.
942	738	Tan–vy. lt. (1 strand)
363	436	Tan (1 strand)
363	436	Tan
370	434	Brown–lt.
371	433	Brown–med.
380	839	Beige Brown–dk.
397	453	Shell Gray–lt.
397	453	Shell Gray–lt. (1 strand)
399	451	Dhell Gray–dk. (1 strand)
399	451	Shell Gray–dk.
401	535	Ash Gray–vy. lt.

Step 2: Backstitch (1 strand)

Anchor	DMC	
881	945	Peach Beige (2 strands)
1019	3802	Antique Mauve–deep (2 strands)
872	3740	Antique Violet–dk.
380	839	Beige Brown–dk.
380	839	Beige Brown–dk. (2 strands)
401	535	Ash Gray–vy. lt.

Step 3: Long Stitch (1 strand)

Anchor	DMC	
387	712	Cream
891	676	Old Gold–lt.
380	839	Beige Brown–dk.
401	535	Ash Gray–vy. lt. (2 strands)

44 Top Left

Stitch Count: 250 width x 162 length

Top Right

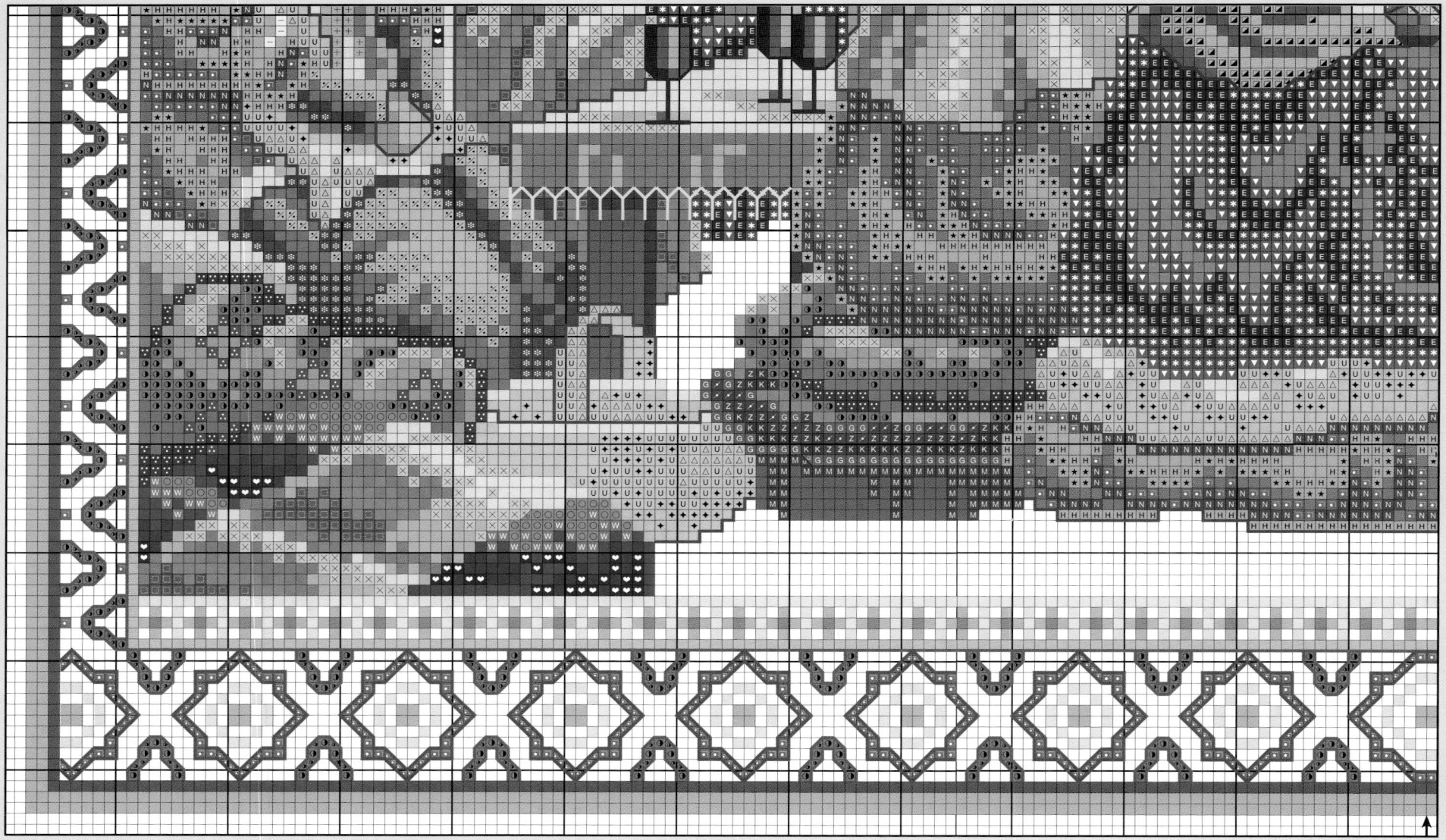

Bottom Left

Bottom Right

Peace

The Lion & the Lamb

The sample was stitched on Cobblestone Cashel Linen 28 over 2. The finished design size is 12⅛" x 7⅞". The fabric was cut 19" x 14".

Anchor	DMC	
Step 1: Cross-stitch (2 strands)		
926		Ecru
886	677	Old Gold–vy. lt.
886	677	Old Gold–vy. lt. (1 strand)
907	3821	Straw (1 strand)
891	676	Old Gold–lt.
890	729	Old Gold–med.
890	729	Old Gold–med. (1 strand)
308	976	Golden Brown–med. (1 strand)
309	782	Topaz–med. (1 strand)
375	420	Hazel Nut Brown–dk. (1 strand)
305	3822	Straw–lt.
306	3820	Straw–dk.
8	353	Peach
9	760	Salmon (1 strand)
10	3712	Salmon–med. (1 strand)
11	3328	Salmon–dk. (1 strand)
897	221	Shell Pink–vy. dk. (1 strand)
75	3733	Dusty Rose–lt.
87	3607	Plum–lt. (1 strand)
69	3687	Mauve (1 strand)
78	3803	Mauve–med.
1019	3802	Antique Mauve–deep (1 strand)
403	310	Black (1 strand)
101	550	Violet–vy. dk. (1 strand)
905	3781	Mocha Brown–dk. (1 strand)
120	794	Cornflower Blue–lt.
121	793	Cornflower Blue–med. (1 strand)
122	3807	Cornflower Blue (1 strand)
940	792	Cornflower Blue–dk.
941	791	Cornflower Blue–vy. dk.
264	472	Avocado Green–ultra lt.
266	471	Avocado Green–vy. lt. (1 strand)
257	3346	Hunter Green (1 strand)
242	989	Forest Green (1 strand)
214	368	Pistachio Green–lt. (1 strand)
214	368	Pistachio Green–lt.
216	367	Pistachio Green–dk. (1 strand)
212	561	Jade–vy. dk. (1 strand)
877	3815	Celadon Green–dk.
877	3815	Celadon Green–dk. (1 strand)
905	3781	Mocha Brown–dk. (1 strand)
862	3362	Pine Green–dk.
879	500	Blue Green–vy. dk. (1 strand)
862	934	Black Avocado Green (1 strand)
888	3828	Hazel Nut Brown
371	433	Brown–med.
357	801	Coffee Brown–dk.
903	640	Beige Gray–vy. dk.
8581	3023	Brown Gray–lt.
273	3787	Brown Gray–dk.
403	310	Black
Step 2: Backstitch (1 strand)		
905	3781	Mocha Brown–dk.
403	310	Black (2 strands)
403	310	Black
Step 3: French Knot (1 strand)		
926		Ecru
905	3781	Mocha Brown–dk.

Stitch Count: 170 width x 110 length

Noah's Ark

The sample was stitched on Driftwood Dublin Linen 25 over 2. The finished design size is 9⅝" x 8⅜". The fabric was cut 16" x 15".

Anchor	DMC	
Step 1:		**Cross-stitch (2 strands)**
1		White
387	712	Cream
293	727	Topaz–vy. lt.
295	726	Topaz–lt. (1 strand)
307	977	Golden Brown–lt. (1 strand)
300	745	Yellow–lt. pale
886	677	Old Gold–vy. lt.
891	676	Old Gold–lt. (1 strand)
890	729	Old Gold–med. (1 strand)
300	745	Yellow–lt. pale (1 strand)
295	726	Topaz–lt. (1 strand)
295	726	Topaz–lt. (1 strand)
307	783	Christmas Gold (1 strand)
307	783	Christmas Gold
11	351	Coral
968	778	Antique Mauve–vy. lt.
108	211	Lavender–lt. (1 strand)
117	3747	Blue Violet–vy. lt. (1 strand)
975	3753	Antique Blue–ultra vy. lt.
920	932	Antique Blue–lt.
121	793	Cornflower Blue–med. (1 strand)
119	333	Blue Violet–vy. dk. (1 strand)
187	958	Seagreen–dk. (1 strand)
1039	3810	Turquoise–dk. (1 strand)
858	524	Fern Green–vy. lt.
859	3052	Green Gray–med.
846	3051	Green Gray–dk.
347	402	Mahogany–vy. lt. (1 strand)
308	976	Golden Brown–med. (1 strand)
355	3826	Golden Brown
370	434	Brown–lt. (1 strand)
382	3021	Brown Gray–vy. dk. (1 strand)
373	422	Hazel Nut Brown–lt.
375	420	Hazel Nut Brown–dk.
375	420	Hazel Nut Brown–dk. (1 strand)
970	315	Antique Mauve–vy. dk. (1 strand)
375	420	Hazel Nut Brown–dk. (1 strand)
307	977	Golden Brown–lt. (1 strand)
375	420	Hazel Nut Brown–dk. (1 strand)
889	610	Drab Brown–vy. dk. (1 strand)
832	612	Drab Brown–med. (1 strand)
898	611	Drab Brown–dk. (1 strand)
898	611	Drab Brown–dk. (1 strand)
888	3828	Hazel Nut Brown–med. (1 strand)
889	610	Drab Brown–vy. dk. (1 strand)
401	844	Beaver Gray–ultra dk. (1 strand)
900	3024	Brown Gray–vy. lt.
382	3021	Brown Gray–vy. dk.
8581	647	Beaver Gray–med.
905	645	Beaver Gray–vy. dk.
401	844	Beaver Gray–ultra dk.
403	310	Black
Step 2:		**Backstitch (1 strand)**
355	3826	Golden Brown
382	3021	Brown Gray–vy. dk.
403	310	Black
Step 3:		**French Knot (1 strand)**
387	712	Cream
888	3828	Hazel Nut Brown–med.
382	3021	Brown Gray–vy. dk.

Stitch Count: 120 width x 105 length

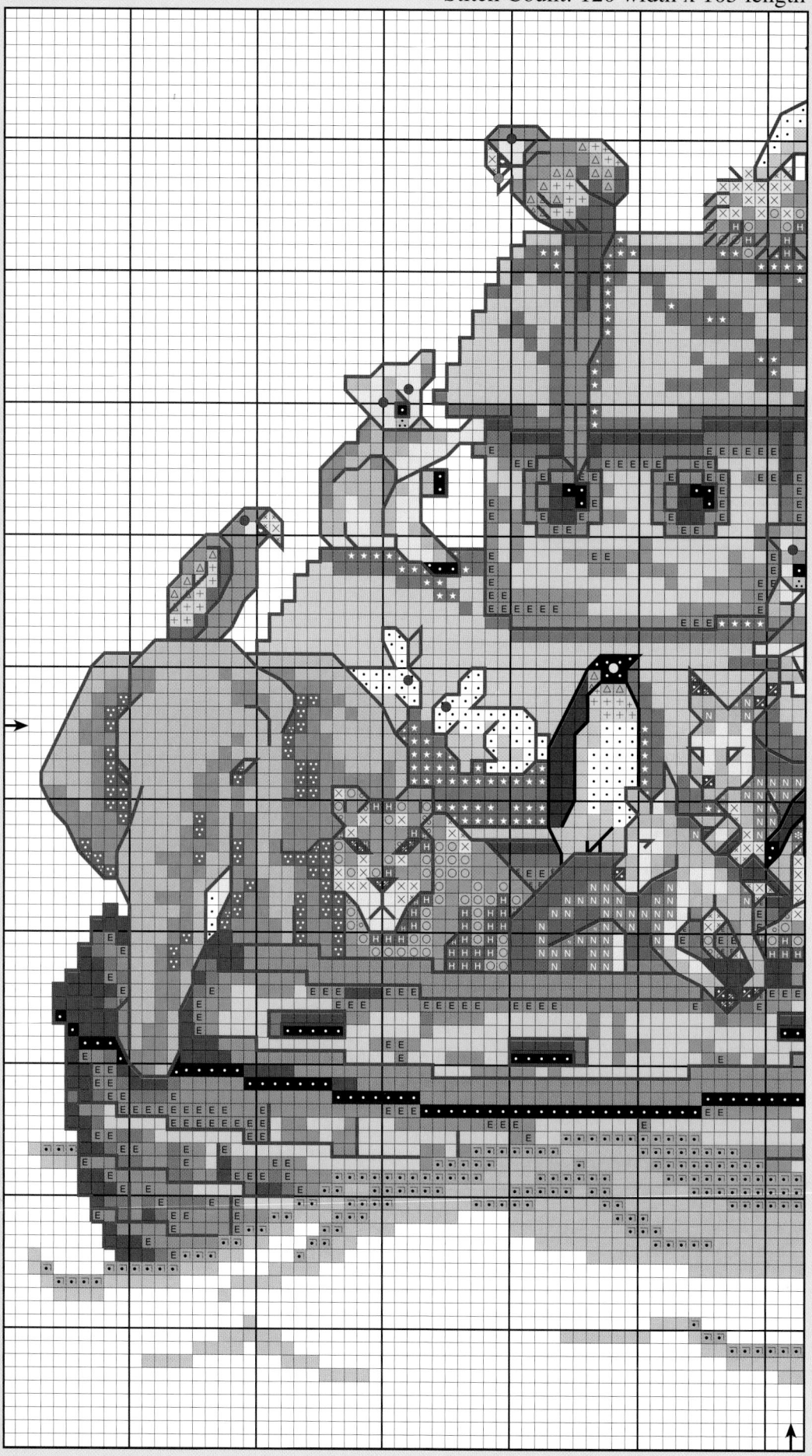

Christmas Play

The sample was stitched on Cameo Rose Cashel Linen 28 over 2. The finished design size is 8⅝" x 7⅞". The fabric was cut 15" x 14".

Anchor **DMC**

Step 1: Cross Stitch (2 strands)

Anchor	DMC	Color
1		White
387	712	Cream
300	745	Yellow–lt. pale
891	676	Old Gold–lt. (1 strand)
881	945	Peach Beige (1 strand)
891	676	Old Gold–lt.
881	945	Peach Beige
10	3712	Salmon–med.
86	3608	Plum–vy. lt.
104	210	Lavender–med.
101	327	Antique Violet–vy. dk.
119	333	Blue Violet–vy. dk.
117	3747	Blue Violet–vy. lt.
145	334	Baby Blue–med.
978	322	Navy Blue–vy. lt.
121	793	Cornflower Blue–med.
858	524	Fern Green–vy. lt.
860	3053	Green Gray
363	436	Tan
375	420	Hazel Nut Brown–dk.
900	3024	Brown Gray–vy. lt.
382	3021	Brown Gray–vy. dk.

Step 2: Backstitch (2 strands)

Anchor	DMC	Color
1		White
387	712	Cream
300	745	Yellow–lt. pale
891	676	Old Gold–lt.
101	327	Antique Violet–vy. dk.
119	333	Blue Violet–vy. dk.
121	793	Cornflower Blue–med.
382	3021	Brown Gray–vy. dk. (1 strand)

Stitch Count: 120 width x 110 length

REPORT CARD
LOVE A
SERVE
RUN

A Good Report

The sample was stitched on Platinum Cashel Linen 28 over 2. The finished design size is 5⅛" x 6⅝". The fabric was cut 12" x 13".

Anchor	DMC	
Step 1: Cross-stitch (2 strands)		
1		White
886	677	Old Gold–vy. lt.
891	676	Old Gold–lt.
306	725	Topaz
366	951	Peach Pecan–lt.
4146	950	Peach Pecan–dk.
11	351	Coral
1014	3830	Terra Cotta–dk.
95	554	Violet–lt.
154	3755	Baby Blue
842	3013	Khaki Green–lt.
373	422	Hazel Nut Brown–lt.
363	436	Tan
388	3033	Mocha Brown–vy. lt.
888	3828	Hazel Nut Brown (1 strand)
379	840	Beige Brown–med. (1 strand)
393	3790	Beige Gray–ultra vy. dk.
900	648	Beaver Gray–lt.
878	501	Blue Green–dk. (1 strand)
401	535	Ash Gray–vy. lt. (1 strand)
Step 2: Backstitch (1 strand)		
1		White (2 strands)
306	725	Topaz
842	3013	Khaki Green–lt. (2 strands)
393	3790	Beige Gray–ultra vy. dk.

A Praying Child

The sample was stitched on Rose Lugana 25 over 2. The finished design size is 5¾" x 7⅜". The fabric was cut 11" x 14".

Anchor	DMC	
Step 1: Cross-stitch (2 strands)		
1		White
886	677	Old Gold–vy. lt.
891	676	Old Gold–lt.
881	945	Peach Beige
881	945	Peach Beige (1 strand)
882	3773	Pecan–vy. lt. (1 strand)
49	963	Wild Rose–vy. lt.
74	3354	Dusty Rose–vy. lt.
66	3688	Mauve–med.
69	3687	Mauve
969	316	Antique Mauve–med.
78	3803	Mauve–dk.
104	210	Lavender–med. (1 strand)
117	3747	Blue Violet–vy. lt. (1 strand)
101	327	Antique Violet–vy. dk.
117	3747	Blue Violet–vy. lt. (1 strand)
1		White (1 strand)
119	333	Blue Violet–vy. dk.
842	3013	Khaki Green–lt.
844	3012	Khaki Green–med.
363	436	Tan (1 strand)
914	3772	Pecan–med. (1 strand)
936	632	Pecan–dk.
Step 2: Backstitch (1 strand)		
936	632	Pecan–dk.
905	3031	Mocha Brown–vy. dk.
Step 3: French Knot (1 strand)		
905	3031	Mocha Brown–vy. dk.

A Good Report – Stitch Count: 72 width x 92 length

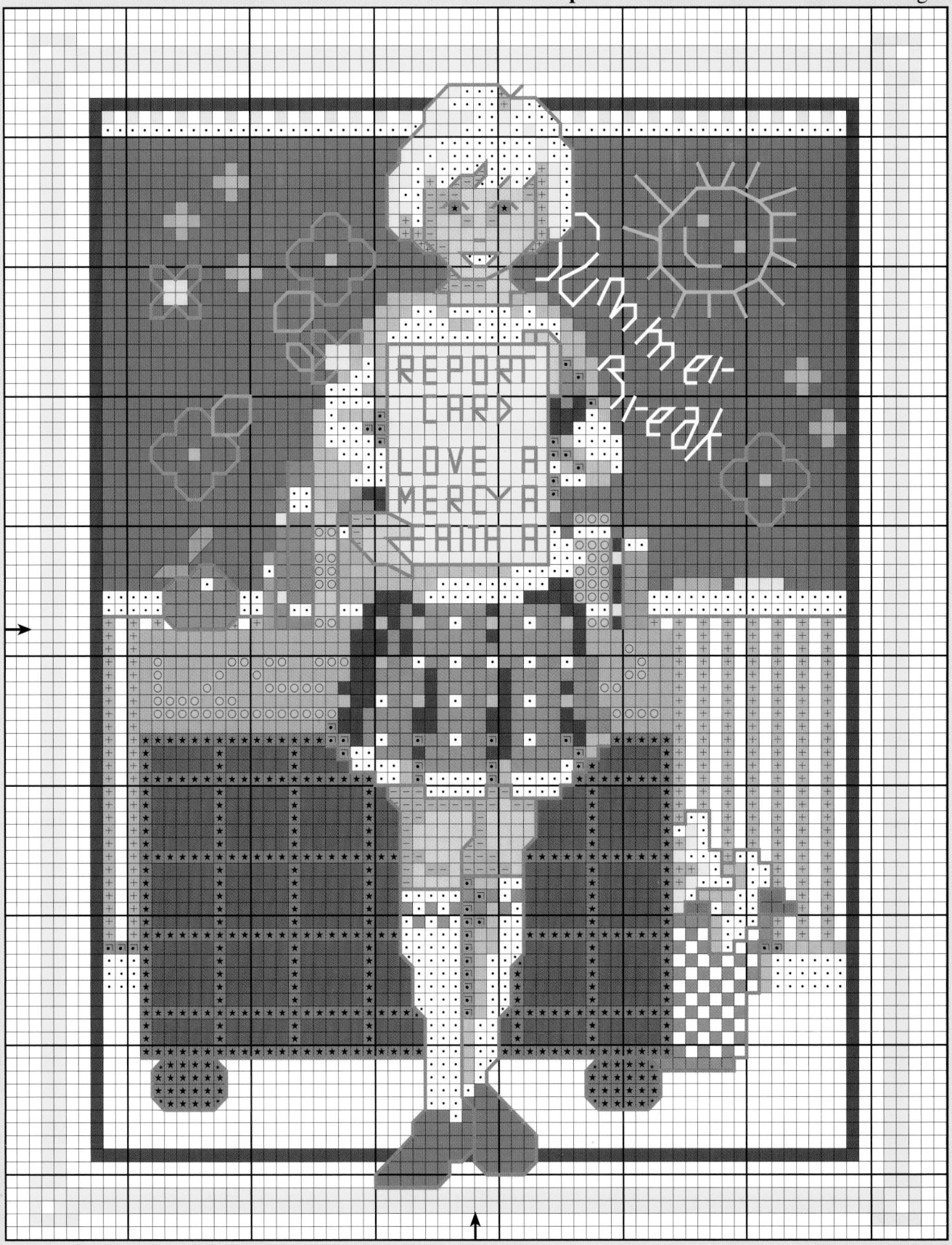

A Praying Child – Stitch Count: 72 width x 92 length

Scripture Reading (see code page 66) – Stitch Count: 72 width x 92 length

Scripture Reading

The sample was stitched on Periwinkle Pastel Linen 28 over 2. The finished design size is 5⅛" x 6⅝". The fabric was cut 12" x 13".

Anchor	DMC	
		Step 1: Cross-stitch (2 strands)
1		White
300	3823	Yellow–ultra pale
301	745	Yellow–pale
891	676	Old Gold–lt.
373	3045	Yellow Beige–dk.
366	951	Peach Pecan–lt.
4146	950	Peach Pecan–dk.
893	224	Shell Pink–lt.
894	223	Shell Pink–med.
970	3726	Antique Mauve–dk.
871	3041	Antique Violet–med. (1 strand)
373	3045	Yellow Beige–dk. (1 strand)
128	800	Delft–pale
159	827	Blue–vy. lt. (1 strand)
160	813	Blue–lt. (1 strand)
161	826	Blue–med.
162	825	Blue–dk.
164	824	Blue–vy. dk.
264	472	Avocado Green–ultra lt.
267	470	Avocado Green–lt.
843	3364	Pine Green
861	3363	Pine Green–med.
862	3362	Pine Green–dk. (1 strand)
267	470	Avocado Green–lt. (1 strand)
874	834	Olive Green–vy. lt.
388	3033	Mocha Brown–vy. lt.
363	436	Tan
309	435	Brown–vy. lt.
900	648	Beaver Gray–lt.
8581	647	Beaver Gray–med.
403	310	Black
		Step 2: Backstitch (1 strand)
393	3790	Beige Gray–ultra vy. dk.
403	310	Black

Santa

See photo, page 69. The sample was stitched on Blue Wing Linen 28 over 2. The finished design size is 8⅝" x 7⅞". The fabric was cut 15" x 14".

Anchor	DMC	
		Step 1: Cross-stitch (2 strands)
1		White
300	3823	Yellow–ultra pale
301	745	Yellow–lt. pale (1 strand)
306	725	Topaz (1 strand)
306	725	Topaz (1 strand)
307	783	Christmas Gold (1 strand)
307	783	Christmas Gold (1 strand)
944	869	Hazel Nut Brown–vy. dk. (1 strand)
4146	754	Peach–lt.
4146	754	Peach–lt. (1 strand)
914	3064	Pecan–lt. (1 strand)
4146	754	Peach–lt. (1 strand)
9	760	Salmon (1 strand)
13	347	Salmon–vy. dk.
47	304	Christmas Red–med.
43	815	Garnet–med.
72	902	Garnet–vy. dk.
104	210	Lavender–med. (1 strand)
105	209	Lavender–dk. (1 strand)
110	208	Lavender–vy. dk.
101	327	Antique Violet–vy. dk.
117	3747	Blue Violet–vy. lt.
117	3747	Blue Violet–vy. lt. (1 strand)
121	793	Cornflower Blue–med. (1 strand)
940	3807	Cornflower Blue
940	792	Cornflower Blue–dk. (1 strand)
101	327	Antique Violet–vy. dk. (1 strand)
158	775	Baby Blue–vy. lt.
158	775	Baby Blue–vy. lt. (1 strand)
	094	Star Blue BF (2 strands)
343	3752	Antique Blue–vy. lt.
343	3752	Antique Blue–vy. lt. (1 strand)
	094	Star Blue BF (2 strands)
920	932	Antique Blue–lt.
920	932	Antique Blue–lt. (1 strand)
	094	Star Blue BF (2 strands)
921	931	Antique Blue–med. (1 strand)
400	414	Steel Gray–dk. (1 strand)

214	368	Pistachio Green–lt. (1 strand)
877	3815	Celadon Green–dk. (1 strand)
212	561	Jade–vy. dk.
879	500	Blue Green–vy. dk.
944	869	Hazel Nut Brown–vy. dk.
397	3072	Beaver Gray–vy. lt.
900	648	Beaver Gray–lt.
8581	647	Beaver Gray–med.
403	310	Black

Step 2: Backstitch (1 strand)

1		White
	032	Pearl Very Fine Braid
	102	Vatican Gold Very Fine Braid
920	932	Antique Blue–lt. (1 strand)
	094	Star Blue BF (1 strand)
944	869	Hazel Nut Brown–vy. dk.
400	414	Steel Gray–dk.
403	310	Black

Step 3: French Knot (1 strand)

43	815	Garnet–med.

Step 4: Long Stitch (1 strand)

032	Pearl Very Fine Braid

Step 5: Stars (1 strand)

1		White
	032	Pearl Very Fine Braid
	102	Vatican Gold Very Fine Braid

Step 6: Wrapped Backstitch

301	745	Yellow–lt. pale (1 strand) (wrap with 002 Gold BF 2 strands)

Step 7: Beadwork

00479	White

Santa – Stitch Count: 120 width x 110 length

KIDS COUNT

Kids Count

The sample was stitched on Toasted Almond Cashel Linen 28 over 2. The finished design size is 12⅛" x 6⅛". The fabric was cut 19" x 13".

Anchor	DMC	
Step 1:	**Cross-stitch (2 strands)**	
1		White
1		White (1 strand)
891	676	Old Gold–lt. (1 strand)
300	745	Yellow–lt. pale
891	676	Old Gold–lt. (1 strand)
306	3820	Straw–dk. (1 strand)
308	782	Topaz–med.
366	951	Peach Pecan–lt.
881	945	Peach Beige
49	963	Wild Rose–vy. lt. (1 strand)
75	604	Cranberry–lt. (1 strand)
75	604	Cranberry–lt. (1 strand)
69	3687	Mauve (1 strand)
69	3687	Mauve (1 strand)
341	3777	Terra Cotta–vy. dk. (1 strand)
896	3722	Shell Pink
44	814	Garnet–dk.
86	3608	Plum–vy. lt.
87	3607	Plum–lt.
78	3803	Mauve–med.
95	554	Violet–lt.
110	208	Lavender–vy. dk.
110	208	Lavender–vy. dk. (1 strand)
940	792	Cornflower Blue–dk. (1 strand)
101	327	Antique Violet–vy. dk.
117	3747	Blue Violet–vy. lt.
117	341	Blue Violet–lt. (1 strand)
118	340	Blue Violet–med. (1 strand)
121	793	Cornflower Blue–med.
940	792	Cornflower Blue–dk.
150	823	Navy Blue–dk.
921	931	Antique Blue–med.
860	3053	Green Gray (1 strand)
266	581	Moss Green (1 strand)
859	3052	Gren Gray–med. (1 strand)
268	937	Avocado Green–med. (1 strand)
379	890	Pistachio Green–ultra dk. (1 strand)
382	3371	Black Brown (1 strand)
311	3827	Golden Brown–pale
307	977	Golden Brown–lt. (1 strand)
888	3828	Hazel Nut Brown (1 strand)
942	738	Tan–vy. lt.
888	3828	Hazel Nut Brown
888	3828	Hazel Nut Brown (1 strand)
370	434	Brown–lt. (1 strand)
944	869	Hazel Nut Brown–vy. dk.
379	840	Beige Brown–med.
380	839	Beige Brown–dk.
360	898	Coffee Brown–vy. dk.
101	327	Antique Violet–vy. dk. (1 strand)
382	3371	Black Brown (1 strand)
8581	646	Beaver Gray–dk.
236	3799	Pewter Gray–vy. dk.

Step 2: Backstitch (1 strand)

1		White
101	327	Antique Violet–vy. dk.
360	898	Coffee Brown–vy. dk.
382	3371	Black Brown

Step 3: French Knot (1 strand)

360	898	Coffee Brown–vy. dk.
382	3371	Black Brown

Stitch Count: 170 width x 86 length

Two by Two

The sample was stitched on Antique White Cashel Linen 28 over 2. The finished design size is 7⅞" x 10¾". The fabric was cut 14" x 17".

Anchor **DMC**

Step 1: Cross-stitch (2 strands)

Anchor	DMC	
1		White
891	676	Old Gold–lt.
307	783	Christmas Gold
868	758	Terra Cotta–lt.
5975	356	Terra Cotta–med.
49	963	Wild Rose–vy. lt.
50	605	Cranberry–vy. lt.
46	666	Christmas Red–bright
897	221	Shell Pink–dk.
22	816	Garnet
871	3041	Antique Violet–med.
167	519	Sky Blue
132	797	Royal Blue
185	964	Seagreen–lt.
186	959	Seagreen–med.
188	3812	Seagreen–vy. dk.
206	955	Nile Green–lt.
204	912	Emerald Green–lt.
205	911	Emerald Green–med.
203	564	Jade–vy. lt.
212	561	Jade–vy. dk.
187	992	Aquamarine
187	992	Aquamarine (1 strand)
878	501	Blue Green–dk. (1 strand)
307	977	Golden Brown–lt.
349	921	Copper
309	435	Brown–vy. lt.
380	839	Beige Brown–dk. (1 strand)
101	550	Violet–vy. dk. (1 strand)
900	648	Beaver Gray–lt.
8581	646	Beaver Gray–dk.
403	310	Black

Step 2: Backstitch (1 strand)

Anchor	DMC	
307	783	Christmas Gold (2 strands)
101	550	Violet–vy. dk.
380	839	Beige Brown–dk.

Step 3: French Knot (1 strand)

Anchor	DMC	
1		White
307	783	Christmas Gold
380	839	Beige Brown–dk.

Step 4: Long Stitch (1 strand)

Anchor	DMC	
307	783	Christmas Gold

Stitch Count: 110 width x 151 length

Top

Bottom

Animal Angels

Puppy Angel

The sample was stitched on Star Sapphire Linen 28 over 2. The finished design size is 5⅜" x 5⅜". The fabric was cut 12" x 12".

Anchor	DMC	
Step 1: Cross-stitch (2 strands)		
1		White
387	712	Cream
886	677	Old Gold–vy. lt.
887	3046	Yellow Beige–med.
373	3045	Yellow Beige–dk.
10	3712	Salmon–med.
42	309	Rose–deep
896	3721	Shell Pink–dk.
1019	3802	Antique Mauve–deep
942	738	Tan–vy. lt. (1 strand)
300	745	Yellow–lt. pale (1 strand)
942	738	Tan–vy. lt. (1 strand)
387	712	Cream (1 strand)
362	437	Tan–lt.
362	437	Tan–lt. (1 strand)
363	436	Tan (1 strand)
309	435	Brown–vy. lt. (1 strand)
349	301	Mahogany–med. (1 strand)
355	975	Golden Brown–dk.
357	801	Coffee Brown–dk.
382	3371	Black Brown
8581	646	Beaver Gray–dk.
Step 2: Backstitch (1 strand)		
363	436	Tan
357	801	Coffee Brown–dk.
382	3371	Black Brown
Step 3: French Knot (1 strand)		
387	712	Cream

Squirrel Angel

The sample was stitched on Potato Annabelle 28 over 2. The finished design size is 4¾" x 5⅝". The fabric was cut 11" x 12".

Anchor	DMC	
Step 1: Cross-stitch (2 strands)		
1		White
387	712	Cream
292	3078	Golden Yellow–vy. lt.
885	739	Tan–ultra vy. lt.
942	738	Tan–vy. lt. (1 strand)
886	677	Old Gold–vy. lt. (1 strand)
373	422	Hazel Nut Brown–lt.
373	422	Hazel Nut Brown–lt. (1 strand)
105	209	Lavender–dk. (1 strand)
956	613	Drab Brown–lt.
832	612	Drab Brown–med.
311	3827	Golden Brown–pale (1 strand)
363	436	Tan (1 strand)
349	301	Mahogany–med. (1 strand)
363	436	Tan (1 strand)
355	975	Golden Brown–dk.
357	801	Coffee Brown–dk.
382	3371	Black Brown
830	644	Beige Gray–med.
8581	647	Beaver Gray–med.
Step 2: Backstitch (1 strand)		
956	613	Drab Brown–lt.
357	801	Coffee Brown–dk.
382	3371	Black Brown
Step 3: French Knot (1 strand)		
1		White
Step 4: Long Stitch (2 strands)		
382	3371	Black Brown

Puppy Angel – Stitch Count: 75 width x 75 length

Squirrel Angel – Stitch Count: 67 width x 78 length

Bear Angel

The sample was stitched on Cameo Rose Cashel Linen 28 over 2. The finished design size is 5¾" x 5⅞". The fabric was cut 12" x 12".

Anchor	DMC	
Step 1: Cross-stitch (2 strands)		
1		White
387	712	Cream
886	677	Old Gold–vy. lt.
301	744	Yellow–pale
887	3046	Yellow Beige–med.
373	3045	Yellow Beige–dk.
366	951	Peach Pecan–lt.
49	3689	Mauve–lt.
66	3688	Mauve–med.
970	3726	Antique Mauve–dk.
869	3743	Antique Violet–vy. lt.
311	3827	Golden Brown–pale
307	977	Golden Brown–lt.
308	3826	Golden Brown
375	420	Hazel Nut Brown–dk.
379	840	Beige Brown–med.
942	738	Tan–vy. lt.
363	436	Tan
309	435	Brown–vy. lt.
371	433	Brown–med.
382	3371	Black Brown
Step 2: Backstitch (1 strand)		
970	3726	Antique Mauve–dk.
1019	3802	Antique Mauve–deep
371	433	Brown–med.
Step 3: French Knot (1 strand)		
387	712	Cream
66	3688	Mauve–med.
382	3371	Black Brown

Bunny Angel

The sample was stitched on Antique Blue Linen 28 over 2. The finished design size is 5¼" x 6". The fabric was cut 12" x 12".

Anchor	DMC	
Step 1: Cross-stitch (2 strands)		
1		White
387	712	Cream
886	677	Old Gold–vy. lt.
887	3046	Yellow Beige–med.
373	3045	Yellow Beige–dk.
366	951	Peach Pecan–lt.
8	761	Salmon–lt.
75	962	Wild Rose–med. (1 strand)
76	3731	Dusty Rose–med. (1 strand)
42	309	Rose–deep
373	422	Hazel Nut Brown–lt.
375	420	Hazel Nut Brown–dk.
942	738	Tan–vy. lt.
363	436	Tan
371	433	Brown–med.
381	938	Coffee Brown–ultra dk.
382	3371	Black Brown
Step 2: Backstitch (1 strand)		
387	712	Cream (2 strands)
	102	Vatican Gold Very Fine Braid
76	3731	Dusty Rose–med.
375	420	Hazel Nut Brown–dk.
381	938	Coffee Brown–ultra dk. (2 strands)
Step 3: French Knot (1 strand)		
1		White
Step 4: Long Stitch (1 strand)		
387	712	Cream

Bear Angel – Stitch Count: 80 width x 82 length

Bunny Angel – Stitch Count: 74 width x 84 length

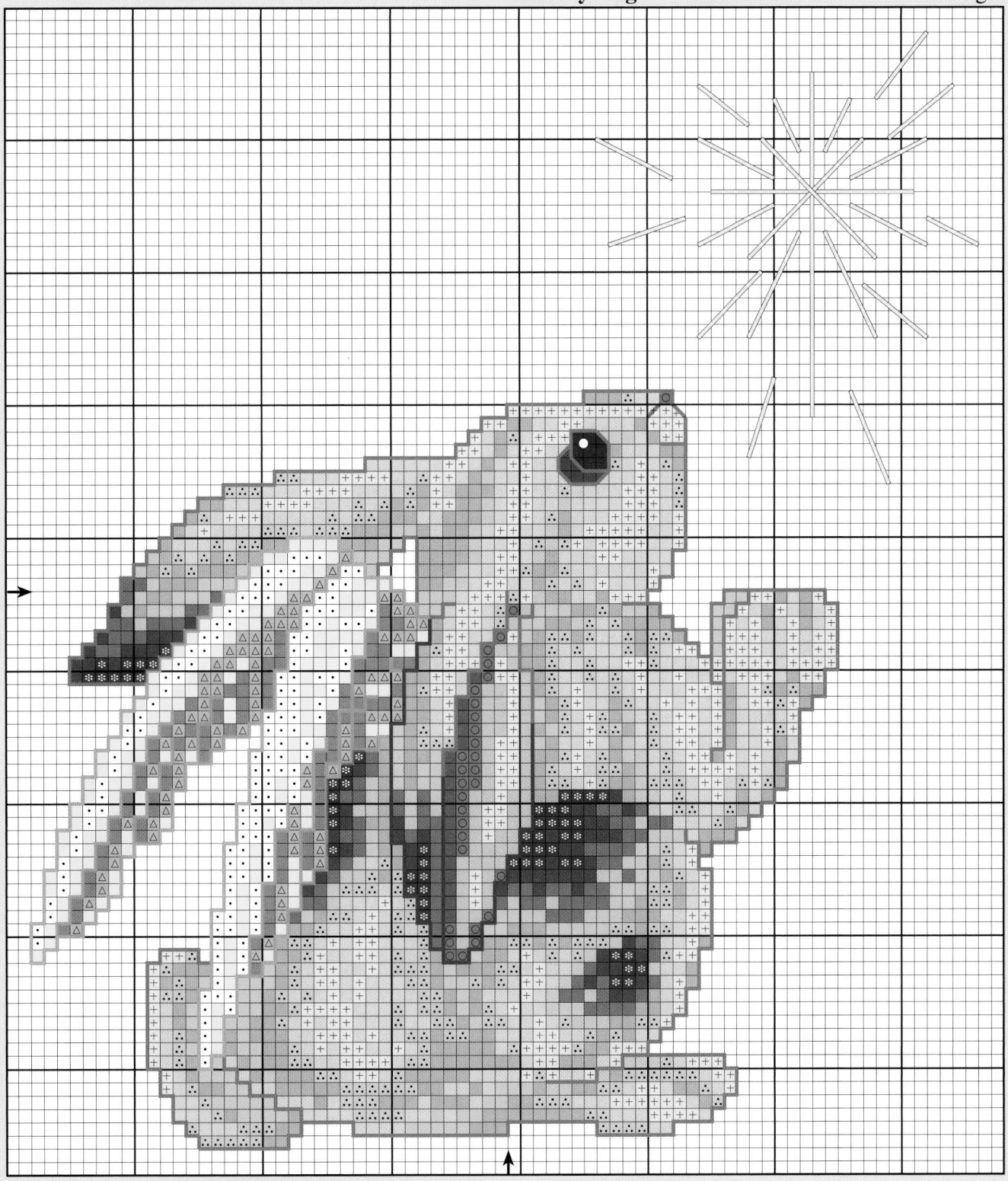

Kitten Angel – Stitch Count: 80 width x 70 length

Kitten Angel

The sample was stitched on Lavender Mist Cashel Linen 28 over 2. The finished design size is 5¾" x 5". The fabric was cut 12" x 12".

Anchor	DMC	
Step 1: Cross-stitch (2 strands)		
1		White
868	3779	Terra Cotta–vy. lt.
337	3778	Terra Cotta
9	760	Salmon
896	3722	Shell Pink
158	3756	Baby Blue–ultra vy. lt.
159	3325	Baby Blue–lt.
779	926	Slate Green
885	739	Tan–ultra vy. lt. (1 strand)
956	613	Drab Brown–lt. (1 strand)
832	612	Drab Brown–med.
388	3033	Mocha Brown–vy. lt.
905	3031	Mocha Brown–vy. dk.
393	3790	Beige Gray–ultra vy. dk.
830	644	Beige Gray–med.
8581	647	Beaver Gray–med.
398	415	Pearl Gray
399	318	Steel Gray–lt.
Step 2: Backstitch (1 strand)		
382	3371	Black Brown (2 strands) (eyes)
382	3371	Black Brown
Step 3: French Knot (1 strand)		
1		White

Angel & Baby

The sample was stitched on Periwinkle Pastel Linen 28 over 2. The finished design size is 4¼" x 5". The fabric was cut 11" x 11".

Anchor	DMC	
Step 1: Cross-stitch (2 strands)		
1		White
300	745	Yellow–lt. pale
886	677	Old Gold–vy. lt.
891	676	Old Gold–lt.
887	3046	Yellow Beige–med.
373	3045	Yellow Beige–dk.
366	951	Peach Pecan–lt.
881	945	Peach Beige
11	3328	Salmon–dk.
49	3689	Mauve–lt.
969	316	Antique Mauve–med.
117	3747	Blue Violet–vy. lt.
118	340	Blue Violet–med.
940	3807	Cornflower Blue
843	3364	Pine Green
311	3827	Golden Brown–pale
363	436	Tan
375	420	Hazel Nut Brown–dk.
899	3782	Mocha Brown–lt.
Step 2: Backstitch (1 strand)		
891	676	Old Gold–lt.
101	327	Antique Violet–vy. dk.
940	3807	Cornflower Blue
843	3364	Pine Green
324	922	Copper–lt. (2 strands)
382	3021	Brown Gray–vy. dk.

Stitch Count: 60 width x 70 length

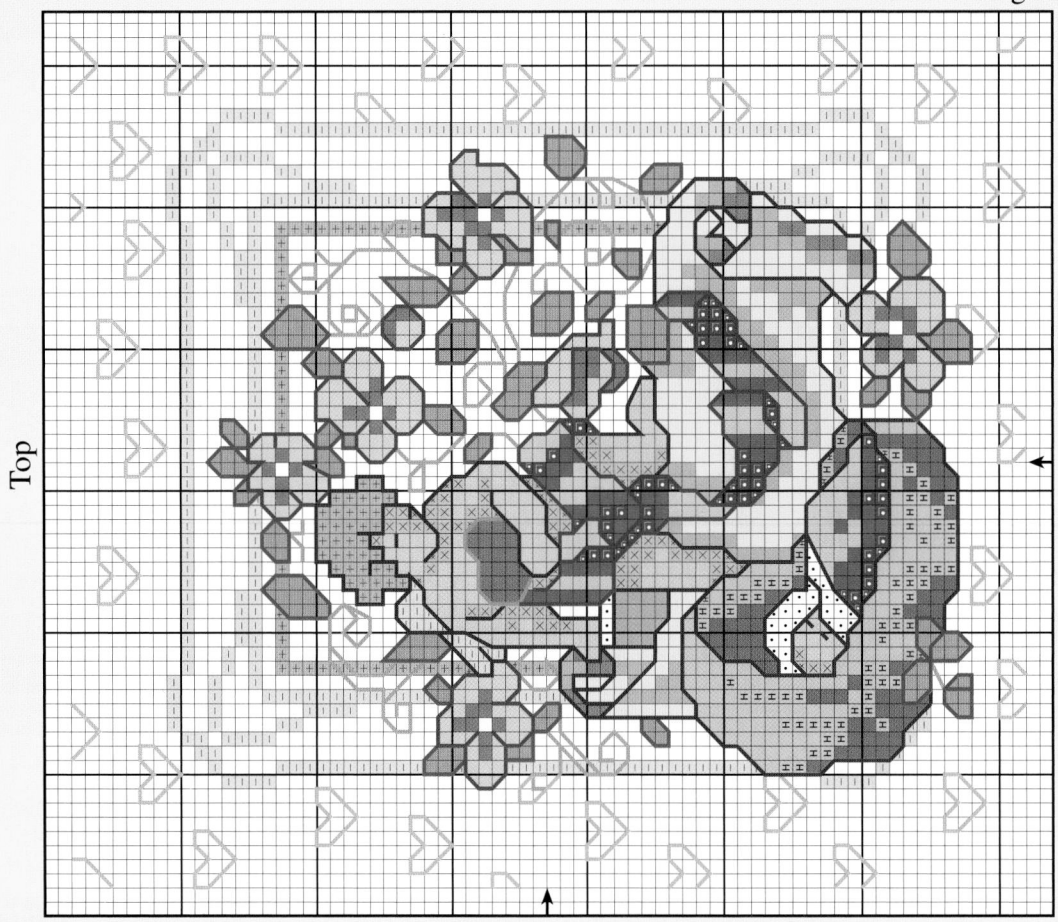

Morning Chorus

The sample was stitched on White Cashel Linen 28 over 2. The finished design size is 4¼" x 5". The fabric was cut 11" x 11".

Anchor **DMC**

Step 1: Cross-stitch (2 strands)

Anchor	DMC	
1		White
300	745	Yellow–lt. pale
306	3820	Straw–dk.
366	951	Peach Pecan–lt.
11	351	Coral
13	349	Coral–dk.
22	816	Garnet
72	902	Garnet–vy. dk.
158	775	Baby Blue–vy. lt.
167	519	Sky Blue
130	799	Delft–med.
843	3364	Pine Green
861	3363	Pine Green–med.
215	320	Pistachio Green–med.
878	501	Blue Green–dk.
830	644	Beige Gray–med.
392	642	Beige Gray–dk.
403	310	Black

Step 2: Backstitch (1 strand)

Anchor	DMC	
306	3820	Straw–dk.
72	902	Garnet–vy. dk.
889	610	Drab Brown–vy. dk.
382	3021	Brown Gray–vy. dk.

Step 3: French Knot (1 strand)

Anchor	DMC	
13	349	Coral–dk.
889	610	Drab Brown–vy. dk.

Stitch Count: 60 width x 70 length

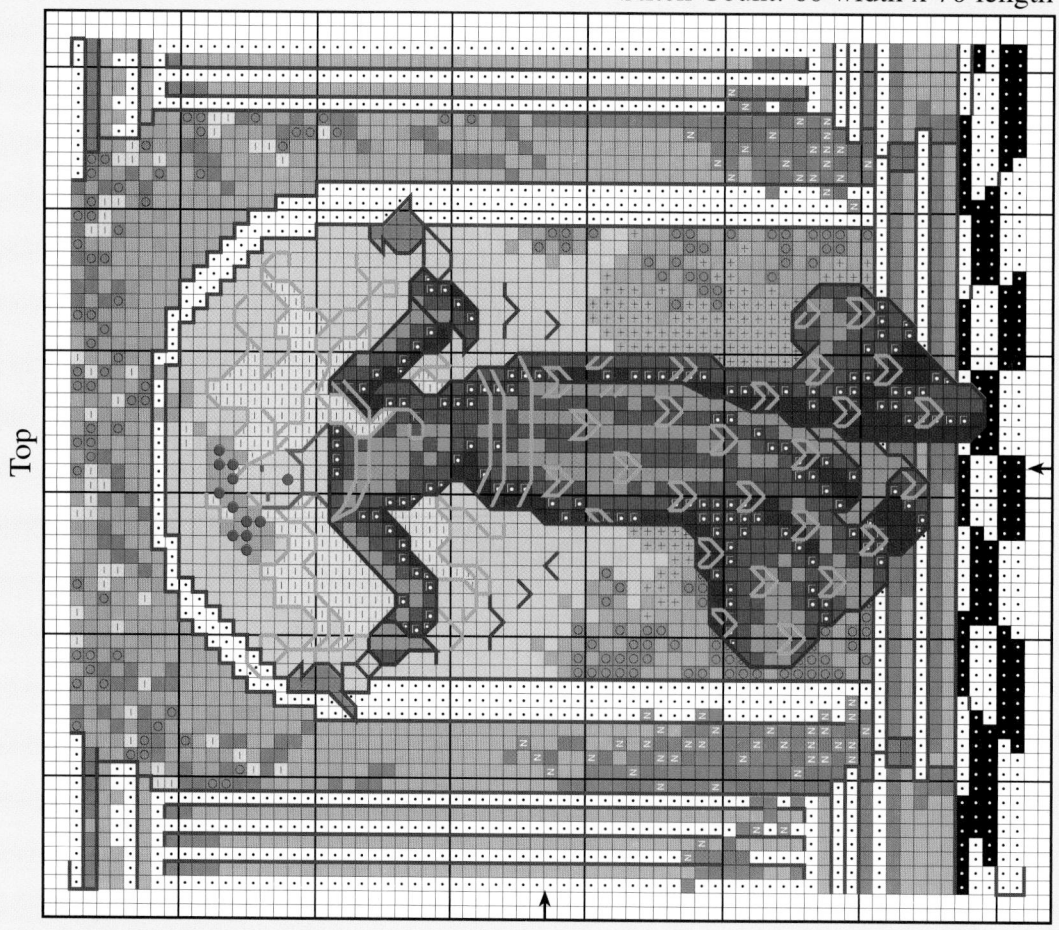

CARPENTER
FAMILY
ALLAN
SMITH
GAIL
SMITH
JEREMMY
TIFFINY
DEBRA
CHOPE
CASSANDRA
ALLYSON
APRIL
ABEL
MALIN
KINSMAN
GARBER
SANDY
BARBER
MILLARY
MADISON
MICHAEL
BARBER
LISA
CARPENTER
JIMMY
GABRIELLA
TRACY
QUIRE
EVELYN
EDWARD
KATHY
LERVY
TAYLOR
SEAN
PAT
CRIN
BARRY
CRIN
MADISON
WENDY
CRIN
RICHARD
SMITH
CORTNEY
RICHARD
WAYNE
SMITH
SELENA
BRIDGET
NANCY
SMITH
KAY
BROWNING
HANNON
JUSTIN
BECKY
NEIGHBORS
DANIEL
SMITH
DANIELLE
WILLIAM
WAYNE
For the LORD is good; His loving kindness is everlasting,
and His faithfulness to all generations. PSALMS 100:5

Family Tree (see code page 94) - Stitch Count: 112 width x 134 length

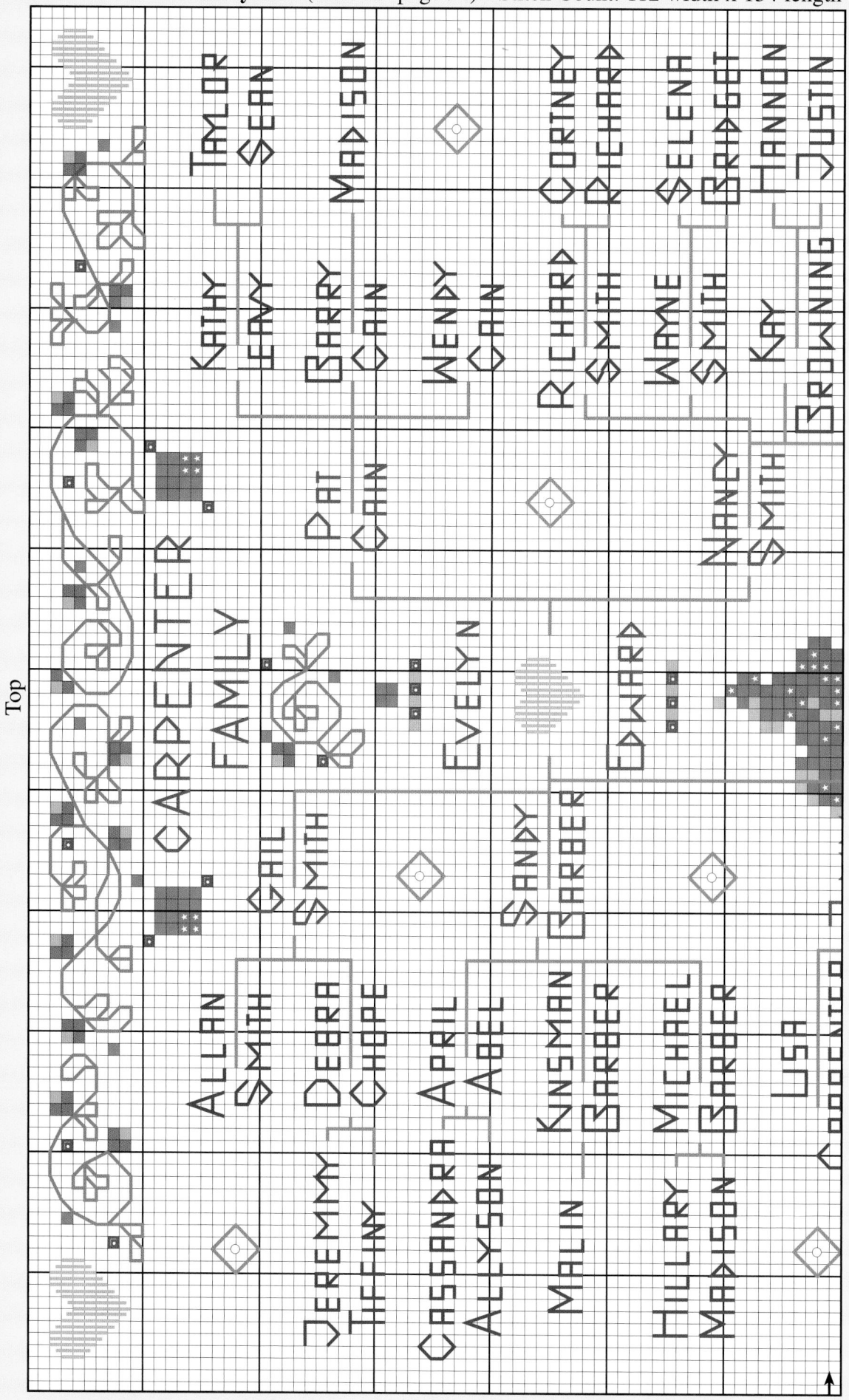

Gabriella
Tracy
Ouore
Carpenter
Becky
Neighbors
Daniel
Smith
Danielle
William
Wayne
For the LORD is good. His loving kindness is everlasting
and His faithfulness to all generations. PSALMS 100:5

Bottom

Family Tree

The sample was stitched on Antique Rose Linen 28 over 2. The finished design size is 8" x 9⅝". The fabric was cut 14" x 16".

Anchor	DMC	
Step 1: Cross-stitch (2 strands)		
891	676	Old Gold–lt.
894	223	Shell Pink–med.
872	3740	Antique Violet–dk.
161	826	Blue–med.
921	931	Antique Blue–med.
900	928	Slate Green–lt.
900	928	Slate Green–lt. (1 strand)
779	926	Slate Green (1 strand)
779	926	Slate Green
388	3033	Mocha Brown–vy. lt.
942	738	Tan–vy. lt.
Step 2: Backstitch (1 strand)		
70	3685	Mauve–dk.
872	3740	Antique Violet–dk. (2 strands) (CARPENTER FAMILY)
872	3740	Antique Violet–dk.
779	926	Slate Green (2 strands)
840	3768	Slate Green–dk.
832	612	Drab Brown–med. (2 strands)
Step 3: French Knot (1 strand)		
840	3768	Slate Green–dk.
Step 4: Long Stitch (1 strand)		
832	612	Drab Brown–med.
Step 5: Satin Stitch (2 strands)		
	91	Blue Varigated
388	3033	Mocha Brown–vy. lt.
Step 6: Beadwork		
	02010	Ice

Little Red Church

See photo, page 1. The sample was stitched on Yellow Pastel Linen 28 over 2. The finished design size is 5⅝" x 5⅞". The fabric was cut 16" x 16".

Anchor	DMC	
Step 1: Cross-stitch (2 strands)		
1		White
893	224	Shell Pink–lt. (1 strand)
894	223	Shell Pink–med. (1 strand)
896	3722	Shell Pink
1019	3802	Antique Mauve–deep
872	3740	Antique Violet–dk.
130	799	Delft–med.
264	472	Avocado Green–ultra lt.
860	3053	Green Gray
214	368	Pistachio Green–lt.
215	320	Pistachio Green–med. (1 strand)
840	3768	Slate Green–dk. (1 strand)
876	502	Blue Green
876	502	Blue Green (1 strand)
266	3347	Yellow Green–med. (1 strand)
878	501	Blue Green–dk.
840	3768	Slate Green–dk.
851	924	Slate Green–vy. dk.
363	436	Tan
370	434	Brown–lt. (1 strand)
393	3790	Beige Gray–ultra vy. dk. (1 strand)
375	420	Hazel Nut Brown–dk.
388	3033	Mocha Brown–vy. lt. (1 strand)
899	3782	Mocha Brown–lt. (1 strand)
905	3781	Mocha Brown–dk.
900	3024	Brown Gray–vy. lt.
8581	647	Beaver Gray–med.
Step 2: Backstitch (1 strand)		
1		White
905	3781	Mocha Brown–dk.
382	3371	Black Brown
Step 3: French Knot (1 strand)		
905	3781	Mocha Brown–dk.
382	3371	Black Brown

Little Red Church - Stitch Count: 78 width x 82 length

Step 4: Long Stitch (2 strands)

1 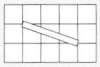 White

FORGIVE
as you hope to be
FORGIVEN
NOEL
REJOICE
Merry Christmas
God Bless Our Home
Make New Friends But Keep the Old One is Silver & the other is Gold.
COME
FIND
PEACE

A Christmas Sampler

The sample was stitched on Mushroom/Gold Lugana 25 over 2. The finished design size is 11½" x 15⅝". The fabric was cut 18" x 22".

Anchor **DMC**

Step 1: Cross Stitch (2 strands)

Anchor	DMC	
1		White
926		Ecru
300	745	Yellow–lt. pale
305	3822	Straw–lt.
886	677	Old Gold–vy. lt.
886	677	Old Gold–vy. lt. (1 strand)
306	725	Topaz (1 strand)
891	676	Old Gold–lt.
891	676	Old Gold–lt. (1 strand)
890	729	Old Gold–med. (1 strand)
890	729	Old Gold–med.
890	729	Old Gold–med. (1 strand)
308	782	Topaz–med. (1 strand)
890	729	Old Gold–med. (1 strand)
375	420	Hazel Nut Brown–dk. (1 strand)
307	783	Christmas Gold
307	783	Christmas Gold (1 strand)
306	725	Topaz (1 strand)
308	782	Topaz–med.
309	781	Topaz–dk.
10	352	Coral–lt.
11	351	Coral
10	3712	Salmon–med.
13	347	Salmon–vy. dk.
892	225	Shell Pink–vy. lt.
893	224	Shell Pink–lt.
894	223	Shell Pink–med. (1 strand)
25	3326	Rose–lt. (1 strand)
896	3722	Shell Pink (1 strand)
27	899	Rose–med. (1 strand)
896	3721	Shell Pink–dk.
49	963	Wild Rose–vy. lt.
49	963	Wild Rose–vy. lt. (1 strand)
8	761	Salmon–lt. (1 strand)
25	3326	Rose–lt. (1 strand)
27	899	Rose–med. (1 strand)
27	899	Rose–med. (1 strand)
896	3722	Shell Pink (1 strand)
74	3354	Dusty Rose–vy. lt. (1 strand)
9	760	Salmon (1 strand)
75	3733	Dusty Rose–lt.
1014	3830	Terra Cotta
22	816	Garnet
44	814	Garnet–dk.
969	316	Antique Mauve–med.
117	3747	Blue Violet–vy. lt.
108	211	Lavender–lt.
108	211	Lavender–lt. (1 strand)
117	341	Blue Violet–lt. (1 strand)
117	341	Blue Violet–lt.
117	341	Blue Violet–lt. (1 strand)
121	793	Cornflower Blue–med. (1 strand)
158	3756	Baby Blue–ultra vy. lt.
158	775	Baby Blue–vy. lt.
159	3325	Baby Blue–lt.
343	3752	Antique Blue–vy. lt.
920	932	Antique Blue–lt.
921	931	Antique Blue–med.
922	930	Antique Blue–dk.
816	3750	Antique Blue–vy. dk.
121	793	Cornflower Blue–med.
940	792	Cornflower Blue–dk.
214	368	Pistachio Green–lt. (1 strand)
265	3348	Yellow Green–lt. (1 strand)
215	320	Pistachio Green–med.
265	3348	Yellow Green–lt.
265	3348	Yellow Green–lt. (1 strand)
843	3364	Pine Green (1 strand)
266	3347	Yellow Green–med.
843	3364	Pine Green
861	3363	Pine Green–med.
861	3363	Pine Green–med. (1 strand)
846	3051	Green Gray–dk. (1 strand)
842	3013	Khaki Green–lt.
842	3013	Khaki Green–lt. (1 strand)
264	472	Avocado Green–ultra lt. (1 strand)
859	3052	Green Gray–dk.
846	3051	Green Gray–dk.
876	502	Blue Green
878	501	Blue Green–dk.
840	3768	Slate Green–dk.
851	924	Slate Green–vy. dk. (1 strand)
846	3051	Green Gray–dk. (1 strand)

373	422	Hazel Nut Brown–lt.
375	420	Hazel Nut Brown–dk.
363	436	Tan
309	435	Brown–vy. lt.
309	435	Brown–vy. lt. (1 strand)
351	400	Mahogany–dk. (1 strand)
351	400	Mahogany–dk.
900	3024	Brown Gray–vy. lt.
388	3033	Mocha Brown–vy. lt.
392	642	Beige Gray–dk.
903	640	Beige Gray–vy. dk.
899	3782	Mocha Brown–lt.
376	842	Beige Brown–vy. lt.
889	610	Drab Brown–vy. dk.
905	3031	Mocha Brown–vy. dk.
236	3799	Pewter Gray–vy. dk.
403	310	Black

Step 2: Backstitch (1 strand)

926		Ecru
307	783	Christmas Gold (2 strands)
308	782	Topaz–med.
309	781	Topaz–dk. (2 strands)
970	3726	Antique Mauve–dk.
1019	3802	Antique Mauve–deep (2 strands)
78	3803	Mauve–dk.
44	814	Garnet–dk. (2 strands)
72	902	Garnet–vy. dk.
872	3740	Antique Violet–dk.
	103	Blue–dk. Varigated
922	930	Antique Blue–dk.
816	3750	Antique Blue–vy. dk.
940	792	Cornflower Blue–dk.
846	3051	Green Gray–dk.
862	935	Avocado Green–dk.
878	501	Blue Green–dk.
840	3768	Slate Green–dk.
851	924	Slate Green–vy. dk.
387	822	Beige Gray–lt. (2 strands)
392	642	Beige Gray–dk.
889	610	Drab Brown–vy. dk.
904	3781	Mocha Brown–dk.
905	3031	Mocha Brown–vy. dk.
236	3799	Pewter Gray–vy. dk.

Step 3: French Knot (1 strand)

926		Ecru
11	350	Coral–med.
969	3727	Antique Mauve–lt.
78	3803	Mauve–dk.
843	3364	Pine Green
	103	Blue–dk. Varigated
889	610	Drab Brown–vy. dk.
904	3781	Mocha Brown–dk.
236	3799	Pewter Gray–vy. dk.

Step 4: Beadwork

02010 Ice

Top Left

Stitch Count: 144 width x 195 length

Top Right

The hardest thing to see is what is not at arm's length
Joy
Love
Gypsy Magic
Carry on folk

Make Some New Friends
But Keep the Old
One is Silver
& the other is Gold.

Bottom Left

Bottom Right

A Floral Sampler

The sampler was not stitched in its entirety. The mini-design of the Floral Tea Towel was stitched on White Aida Tea Towel 14 over 1. The finished design size is 3¼" x 1⅜".

Anchor DMC

Step 1: Cross-stitch (2 strands)

Anchor	DMC	
1		White
926		Ecru
300	3823	Yellow–ultra pale
300	745	Yellow–lt. pale
305	3822	Straw–lt.
907	3821	Straw
306	3820	Straw–dk.
886	677	Old Gold–vy. lt.
891	676	Old Gold–lt.
891	676	Old Gold–lt. (1 strand)
300	745	Yellow–lt. pale (1 strand)
890	729	Old Gold–med.
307	783	Christmas Gold
886	3047	Yellow Beige–lt.
881	945	Peach Beige
8	761	Salmon–lt.
11	3328	Salmon–dk.
10	352	Coral–lt.
11	351	Coral
11	350	Coral–med. (1 strand)
896	3721	Shell Pink–dk. (1 strand)
892	225	Shell Pink–vy. lt.
892	225	Shell Pink–vy. lt. (1 strand)
8	761	Salmon–lt. (1 strand)
893	224	Shell Pink–lt.
893	224	Shell Pink–lt. (1 strand)
894	223	Shell Pink–med. (1 strand)
894	223	Shell Pink–med.
896	3722	Shell Pink
49	963	Wild Rose–vy. lt.
49	963	Wild Rose–vy. lt. (1 strand)
108	211	Lavender–lt. (1 strand)
25	3326	Rose–lt.
25	3326	Rose–lt. (1 strand)
27	899	Rose–med. (1 strand)
969	3727	Antique Mauve–lt.
969	316	Antique Mauve–med.
969	316	Antique Mauve–med. (1 strand)
8	761	Salmon–lt. (1 strand)
970	3726	Antique Mauve–dk. (1 strand)
69	3687	Mauve (1 strand)
108	211	Lavender–lt.
104	210	Lavender–med.
104	210	Lavender–med. (1 strand)
108	211	Lavender–lt. (1 strand)
870	3042	Antique Violet–lt.
870	3042	Antique Violet–lt. (1 strand)
118	340	Blue Violet–med. (1 strand)
871	3041	Antique Violet–med.
872	3740	Antique Violet–dk. (1 strand)
110	208	Lavender–vy. dk. (1 strand)
117	3747	Blue Violet–vy. lt.
117	3747	Blue Violet–vy. lt. (1 strand)
158	775	Baby Blue–vy. lt. (1 strand)
117	341	Blue Violet–lt.
117	341	Blue Violet–lt. (1 strand)
104	210	Lavender–med. (1 strand)
117	341	Blue Violet–lt. (1 strand)
118	340	Blue Violet–med. (1 strand)
118	340	Blue Violet–med.
160	3761	Sky Blue–lt.
167	519	Sky Blue
158	775	Baby Blue–vy. lt.
159	3325	Baby Blue–lt.
975	3753	Antique Blue–ultra vy. lt.
121	793	Cornflower Blue–med.
940	792	Cornflower Blue–dk.
940	792	Cornflower Blue–dk. (1 strand)
118	340	Blue Violet–med. (1 strand)
876	502	Blue Green
878	501	Blue Green–dk.
878	501	Blue Green–dk. (1 strand)
861	3363	Pine Green–med. (1 strand)
779	926	Slate Green
840	3768	Slate Green–dk.
859	522	Fern Green
843	3364	Pine Green
843	3364	Pine Green (1 strand)
264	472	Avocado Green–ultra lt. (1 strand)
861	3363	Pine Green–med.
861	3363	Pine Green–med. (1 strand)
266	3347	Yellow Green–med. (1 strand)

264	472	Avocado Green–ultra lt.
859	3052	Green Gray–med.
265	3348	Yellow Green–lt.
842	3013	Khaki Green–lt. (1 strand)
267	470	Avocado Green–lt. (1 strand)
844	3012	Khaki Green–med.
215	3aa20	Pistachio Green–med.
246	319	Pistachio Green–vy. dk.
311	3827	Golden Brown–pale
307	977	Golden Brown–lt.
832	612	Drab Brown–med.
373	422	Hazel Nut Brown–lt.
375	420	Hazel Nut Brown–dk.
375	420	Hazel Nut Brown–dk. (1 strand)
373	422	Hazel Nut Brown–lt. (1 strand)
944	869	Hazel Nut Brown–vy. dk.
899	3782	Mocha Brown–lt.
403	310	Black

Step 2: Backstitch (1 strand)

897	221	Shell Pink–vy. dk.
	52	Purple Varigated
969	316	Antique Mauve–med.
970	315	Antique Mauve–vy. dk.
1019	3802	Antique Mauve–deep

872	3740	Antique Violet–dk.
922	930	Antique Blue–dk.
121	793	Cornflower Blue–med.
878	501	Blue Green–dk.
851	924	Slate Green–vy. dk.
846	3051	Green Gray–dk.
269	936	Avocado Green–dk.
862	935	Avocado Green–vy. dk.
246	319	Pistachio Green–vy. dk.
905	3781	Mocha Brown–dk.
905	3031	Mocha Brown–vy. dk.
382	3021	Brown Gray–vy. dk.

Step 3: French Knot (1 strand)

892	225	Shell Pink–vy. lt.
922	930	Antique Blue–dk.
905	3781	Mocha Brown–dk.

Step 4: Beadwork

00151	Ash Mauve
00358	Cobalt Blue

Top Left

Stitch Count: 145 width x 199 length

Those who
plant kindness
Harvest love

To every thing
there is a season
and a time to every purpose
under the heaven.
Eccl. 3:1

Bottom Left

Bottom Right

A Winter Sampler

The sampler was not stitched in its entirety. The mini-design of Santa with the animals was stitched on White Cashel Linen 28 over 2. The finished design size is 2¾" x 3⅜". The fabric was cut 9" x 10".

Step 1: Cross-stitch (2 strands)

Anchor	DMC	
1		White
926		Ecru
300	745	Yellow–lt. pale
305	3822	Straw–lt.
907	3821	Straw
306	3820	Straw–dk.
886	677	Old Gold–vy. lt.
886	677	Old Gold–vy. lt. (1 strand)
386	746	Off White (1 strand)
891	676	Old Gold–lt.
890	729	Old Gold–med.
373	3045	Yellow Beige–dk.
307	783	Christmas Gold
307	783	Christmas Gold (1 strand)
306	725	Topaz (1 strand)
881	945	Peach Beige
4146	754	Peach–lt.
324	721	Orange Spice–med.
9	760	Salmon
10	3712	Salmon–med.
11	3328	Salmon–dk.
13	347	Salmon–vy. dk.
10	351	Coral
11	350	Coral–med.
20	498	Christmas Red–dk.
22	816	Garnet
49	963	Wild Rose–vy. lt.
25	3326	Rose–lt.
27	899	Rose–med.
42	335	Rose
76	3731	Dusty Rose–med.
892	225	Shell Pink–vy. lt.
894	223	Shell Pink–med.
75	604	Cranberry–lt.
69	3687	Mauve
78	3803	Mauve–dk.
969	316	Antique Mauve–med.
970	315	Antique Mauve–vy. dk.
86	3608	Plum–vy. lt.
87	3607	Plum–lt.
88	718	Plum
108	211	Lavender–lt.
104	210	Lavender–med.
871	3041	Antique Violet–med.
872	3740	Antique Violet–dk.
117	3747	Blue Violet–vy. lt.
117	3747	Blue Violet–vy. lt. (1 strand)
1		White (1 strand)
117	341	Blue Violet–lt.
118	340	Blue Violet–med.
118	340	Blue Violet–med. (1 strand)
117	3747	Blue Violet–vy. lt. (1 strand)
119	333	Blue Violet–vy. dk.
158	775	Baby Blue–vy. lt.
159	3325	Baby Blue–lt.
121	794	Cornflower Blue–lt.
121	793	Cornflower Blue–med.
940	3807	Cornflower Blue
130	799	Delft–med.
131	798	Delft–dk.
132	797	Royal Blue
975	3753	Antique Blue–ultra vy. lt.
922	930	Antique Blue–dk.
167	519	Sky Blue
167	3766	Peacock Blue–lt.
214	368	Pistachio Green–lt.
208	563	Jade–lt.
279	734	Olive Green–lt.
266	581	Moss Green
858	524	Fern Green–vy. lt.
843	3364	Pine Green
843	3364	Pine Green (1 strand)
266	471	Avocado Green–vy. lt. (1 strand)
861	3363	Pine Green–med.
859	3052	Green Gray–med.
266	3347	Yellow Green–med.
876	502	Blue Green
878	501	Blue Green–dk.
877	3815	Celadon Green–dk.
387	822	Beige Gray–lt.
324	922	Copper–lt.

338	3776	Mahogany–lt.
942	738	Tan–vy. lt.
362	437	Tan–lt.
363	436	Tan
309	435	Brown–vy. lt.
388	3033	Mocha Brown–vy. lt.
899	3782	Mocha Brown–lt.
373	422	Hazel Nut Brown–lt.
956	613	Drab Brown–lt.
832	612	Drab Brown–med.
898	611	Drab Brown–dk.
888	3828	Hazel Nut Brown
936	632	Pecan–dk.
376	842	Beige Brown–vy. lt.
1014	3830	Terra Cotta
382	3371	Black Brown
830	644	Beige Gray–med.
397	3072	Beaver Gray–vy. lt.
900	648	Beaver Gray–lt.
8581	647	Beaver Gray–med.
900	3024	Brown Gray–vy. lt.
8581	3022	Brown Gray–med.
397	762	Pearl Gray–vy. lt.
398	415	Pearl Gray
403	310	Black

Step 2: Backstitch (1 strand)

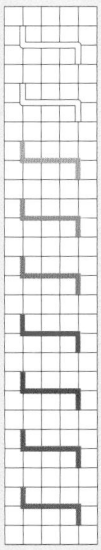

1		White
926		Ecru
306	3820	Straw–dk.
307	783	Christmas Gold
11	3328	Salmon–dk.
89	917	Plum–med.
78	3803	Mauve–dk.
872	3740	Antique Violet–dk.
121	793	Cornflower Blue–med.

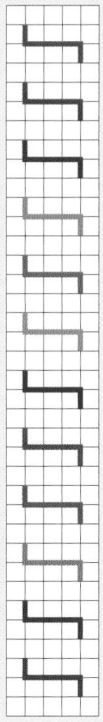

940	3807	Cornflower Blue
940	792	Cornflower Blue–dk.
941	791	Cornflower Blue–vy. dk.
862	520	Fern Green–dk.
862	3362	Pine Green–dk.
876	502	Blue Green
246	319	Pistachio Green–vy. dk.
905	3781	Mocha Brown–dk.
889	610	Drab Brown–vy. dk.
393	3790	Beige Gray–ultra vy. dk.
382	3021	Brown Gray–vy. dk.
401	844	Beaver Gray–ultra dk.

Step 3: French Knot (1 strand)

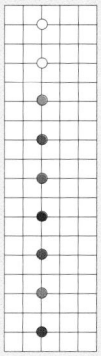

1		White
926		Ecru
324	721	Orange Spice–med.
13	349	Coral–dk.
118	340	Blue Violet–med.
382	3371	Black Brown
905	3781	Mocha Brown–dk.
393	3790	Beige Gray–ultra vy. dk.
382	3021	Brown Gray–vy. dk.

Step 4: Long Stitch (1 strand)

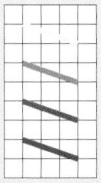

926		Ecru
307	783	Christmas Gold
872	3740	Antique Violet–dk.
905	3781	Mocha Brown–dk.

Step 5: Beadwork

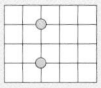

02010	Ice
02011	Victorian Gold

Top Left Stitch Count: 138 width x 186 length

Top Right

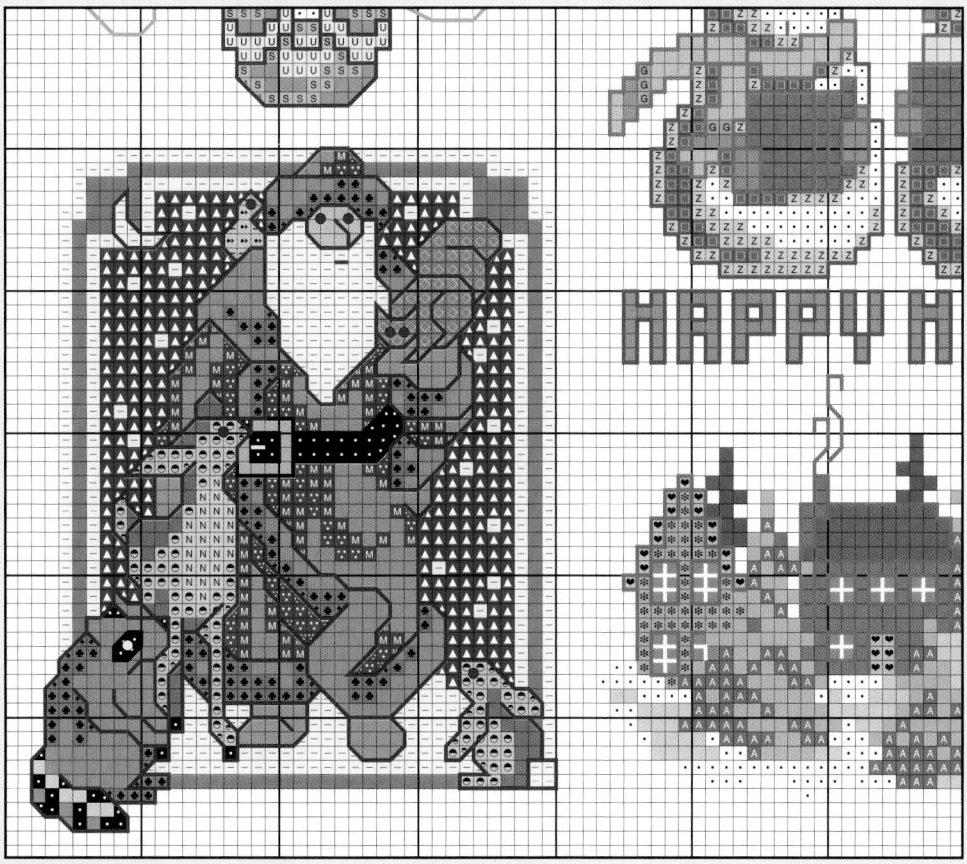

Bottom Left

Bottom Right

Listening
Hearts
Hear Angels
Sing

A Bear Sampler

The sampler was not stitched in its entirety. The mini-design of the angel with verse was stitched on Cream Silk Canvas 24 over 2. The finished design size is 3¾" x 4¼". The fabric was cut 10" x 11". The floral heart was stitched on Cream Cashel Linen 28 over 2. The finished design size is 2⅞" x 2½". The fabric was cut fabric 9" x 9".

Anchor	DMC	
Step 1:		**Cross-stitch (2 strands)**
1		White
926		Ecru
387	712	Cream
387	712	Cream (1 strand)
117	3747	Blue Violet–vy. lt. (1 strand)
386	746	Off White (1 strand)
300	745	Yellow–lt. pale (1 strand)
300	745	Yellow–lt. pale
306	725	Topaz
907	3821	Straw
886	677	Old Gold–vy. lt.
886	677	Old Gold–vy. lt. (1 strand)
891	676	Old Gold–lt. (1 strand)
891	676	Old Gold–lt.
890	729	Old Gold–med.
307	783	Christmas Gold
881	945	Peach Beige
49	963	Wild Rose–vy. lt.
25	3326	Rose–lt.
25	3326	Rose–lt. (1 strand)
9	760	Salmon (1 strand)
27	899	Rose–med. (1 strand)
76	3731	Dusty Rose–med. (1 strand)
8	761	Salmon–lt.
9	760	Salmon
10	3712	Salmon–med.
10	3712	Salmon–med. (1 strand)
894	223	Shell Pink–med. (1 strand)
11	3328	Salmon–dk.
11	351	Coral
894	223	Shell Pink–med.
896	3722	Shell Pink
897	221	Shell Pink–vy. dk.
85	3609	Plum–ultra lt. (1 strand)
66	3688	Mauve–med. (1 strand)
87	3607	Plum–lt. (1 strand)
69	3687	Mauve (1 strand)
49	3689	Mauve–lt. (1 strand)
969	3727	Antique Mauve–lt. (1 strand)
66	3688	Mauve–med.
69	3687	Mauve
78	3803	Mauve–dk.
78	3803	Mauve–dk. (1 strand)
101	327	Antique Violet–vy. dk. (1 strand)
969	316	Antique Mauve–med.
108	211	Lavender–lt.
117	3747	Blue Violet–vy. lt.
872	3740	Antique Violet–dk.
101	327	Antique Violet–vy. dk.
158	3756	Baby Blue–ultra vy. lt.
158	3756	Baby Blue–ultra vy. lt. (1 strand)
128	800	Delft–pale (1 strand)
158	775	Baby Blue–vy. lt.
158	775	Baby Blue–vy. lt. (1 strand)
159	3325	Baby Blue–lt. (1 strand)
158	775	Baby Blue–vy. lt. (1 strand)
128	800	Delft–pale (1 strand)
159	3325	Baby Blue–lt.
154	3755	Baby Blue
154	3755	Baby Blue (1 strand)
145	334	Baby Blue–med. (1 strand)
145	334	Baby Blue–med.
128	800	Delft–pale
121	794	Cornflower Blue–lt.
978	322	Navy Blue–vy. lt. (1 strand)
921	931	Antique Blue–med. (1 strand)
978	322	Navy Blue–vy. lt. (1 strand)
147	312	Navy Blue–lt. (1 strand)
921	931	Antique Blue–med.
132	797	Royal Blue
149	311	Navy Blue–med.
185	964	Seagreen–lt.
849	927	Slate Green–med.
779	926	Slate Green
840	3768	Slate Green–dk.
840	3768	Slate Green–dk. (1 strand)
879	500	Blue Green–vy. dk. (1 strand)

858	524	Fern Green–vy. lt.
859	523	Fern Green–lt.
859	522	Fern Green
842	3013	Khaki Green–lt.
844	3012	Khaki Green–med.
265	3348	Yellow Green–lt.
265	3348	Yellow Green–lt. (1 strand)
843	3364	Pine Green (1 strand)
215	320	Pistachio Green–med.
264	472	Avocado Green–ultra lt.
859	3052	Green Gray–med.
843	3364	Pine Green
861	3363	Pine Green–med.
861	3363	Pine Green–med. (1 strand)
876	502	Blue Green (1 strand)
217	3817	Celadon Green–lt.
213	504	Blue Green–lt.
876	502	Blue Green
311	3827	Golden Brown–pale
307	977	Golden Brown–lt.
347	402	Mahogany–vy. lt.
338	3776	Mahogany–lt.
338	3776	Mahogany–lt. (1 strand)
309	435	Brown–vy. lt. (1 strand)
362	437	Tan–lt.
363	436	Tan
363	436	Tan (1 strand)
309	435	Brown–vy. lt. (1 strand)
370	434	Brown–lt.
373	422	Hazel Nut Brown–lt.
373	422	Hazel Nut Brown–lt. (1 strand)
890	729	Old Gold–med. (1 strand)
888	3828	Hazel Nut Brown
375	420	Hazel Nut Brown–dk.
375	420	Hazel Nut Brown–dk. (1 strand)
890	729	Old Gold–med. (1 strand)
832	612	Drab Brown–med. (1 strand)
898	611	Drab Brown–dk. (1 strand)
388	3033	Mocha Brown–vy. lt. (1 strand)
900	3024	Brown Gray–vy. lt. (1 strand)
905	3031	Mocha Brown–vy. dk. (1 strand)
273	3787	Brown Gray–dk. (1 strand)
376	842	Beige Brown–vy. lt.
378	841	Beige Brown–lt.
379	840	Beige Brown–med.
382	3371	Black Brown
387	822	Beige Gray–lt.
900	648	Beaver Gray–lt.

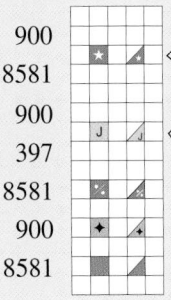

900	648	Beaver Gray–lt. (1 strand)
8581	647	Beaver Gray–med. (1 strand)
900	648	Beaver Gray–lt. (1 strand)
397	3072	Beaver Gray–vy. lt. (1 strand)
8581	647	Beaver Gray–med.
900	3024	Brown Gray–vy. lt.
8581	3023	Brown Gray–lt.

Step 2: Backstitch (1 strand)

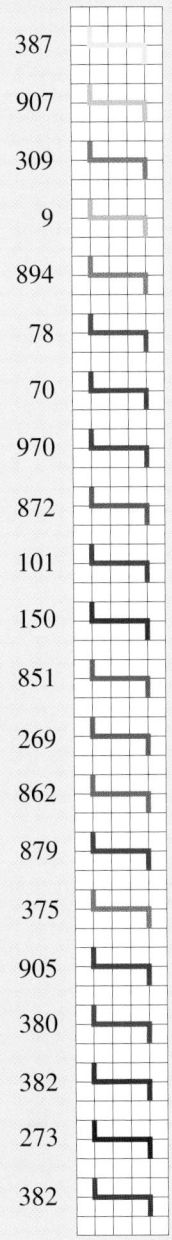

387	712	Cream
907	3821	Straw
309	781	Topaz–dk.
9	760	Salmon
894	223	Shell Pink–med.
78	3803	Mauve–dk.
70	3685	Mauve–vy. dk.
970	315	Antique Mauve–vy. dk.
872	3740	Antique Violet–dk.
101	327	Antique Violet–vy. dk.
150	823	Navy Blue–dk.
851	924	Slate Green–vy. dk.
269	936	Avocado Green–vy. dk.
862	3362	Pine Green–dk.
879	500	Blue Green–vy. dk.
375	420	Hazel Nut Brown–dk.
905	3031	Mocha Brown–vy. dk.
380	839	Beige Brown–dk.
382	3371	Black Brown
273	3787	Brown Gray–dk.
382	3021	Brown Gray–vy. dk.

Step 3: French Knot (1 strand)

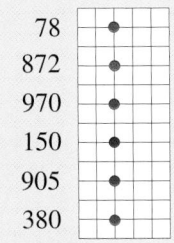

78	3803	Mauve–dk.
872	3740	Antique Violet–dk.
970	315	Antique Mauve–vy. dk.
150	823	Navy Blue–dk.
905	3031	Mocha Brown–vy. dk.
380	839	Beige Brown dk.

Top Left

Stitch Count: 140 width x 191 length

382	•	3021	Brown Gray–vy. dk.

Step 4: Long Stitch (1 strand)

1			White
309		781	Topaz–dk.

Top Right

Bottom Left

Bottom Right

An Alphabet Sampler

The sampler was not stitched in its entirety. The mini-design of the Peace of Earth Angel was stitched on Pearly Grey Cashel Linen 28 over 2. The finished design size is 2¾" x 4". The fabric was cut 9" x 10".

Anchor DMC

Step 1: Cross-stitch (2 strands)

Anchor	DMC	
1		White
387	712	Cream
300	745	Yellow–lt. pale
886	677	Old Gold–vy. lt.
891	676	Old Gold–lt.
907	3821	Straw
307	783	Christmas Gold
307	783	Christmas Gold (1 strand)
306	725	Topaz (1 strand)
308	782	Topaz–med.
366	951	Peach Beige–lt.
881	945	Peach Beige
881	945	Peach Beige (1 strand)
882	3773	Pecan–vy. lt. (1 strand)
48	818	Baby Pink
49	963	Wild Rose–vy. lt.
49	963	Wild Rose–vy. lt. (1 strand)
85	3609	Plum–ultra lt. (1 strand)
24	776	Pink–med.
25	3326	Rose–lt.
25	3326	Rose–lt. (1 strand)
27	899	Rose–med. (1 strand)
25	3326	Rose–lt. (1 strand)
894	223	Shell Pink–med. (1 strand)
27	899	Rose–med.
76	3731	Dusty Rose–med.
10	3712	Salmon–med.
11	3328	Salmon–dk.
11	351	Coral
49	3689	Mauve–lt. (1 strand)
66	3688	Mauve–med. (1 strand)
66	3688	Mauve–med.
66	3688	Mauve–med. (1 strand)
105	209	Lavender–dk. (1 strand)
69	3687	Mauve
69	3687	Mauve (1 strand)
86	3608	Plum–vy. lt. (1 strand)
69	3687	Mauve (1 strand)
970	3726	Antique Mauve–dk. (1 strand)
70	3685	Mauve–vy. dk. (1 strand)
86	3608	Plum–vy. lt.
894	223	Shell Pink–med.
896	3722	Shell Pink
1014	3830	Terra Cotta (1 strand)
970	3726	Antique Mauve–dk.
78	3803	Mauve–dk.
108	211	Lavender–lt.
105	209	Lavender–dk.
95	554	Violet–lt.
95	554	Violet–lt. (1 strand)
118	340	Blue Violet–med. (1 strand)
99	552	Violet–dk.
871	3041	Antique Violet–med.
871	3041	Antique Violet–med. (1 strand)
119	333	Blue Violet–vy. dk. (1 strand)
872	3740	Antique Violet–dk.
117	3747	Blue Violet–vy. lt.
119	3746	Blue Violet–dk.
119	333	Blue Violet–vy. dk.
158	3756	Baby Blue–ultra vy. lt.
158	775	Baby Blue–vy. lt.
128	800	Delft–pale
154	3755	Baby Blue
978	322	Navy Blue–vy. lt.
121	793	Cornflower Blue–med.
940	3807	Cornflower Blue
185	964	Seagreen–lt.
779	926	Slate Green
265	3348	Yellow Green–lt.
842	3013	Khaki Green–lt.
842	3013	Khaki Green–lt. (1 strand)
844	3012	Khaki Green–med. (1 strand)
844	3012	Khaki Green–med.
843	3364	Pine Green
843	3364	Pine Green (1 strand)
861	3363	Pine Green–med. (1 strand)
861	3363	Pine Green–med.
862	3362	Pine Green–dk.

862	3362	Pine Green–dk. (1 strand)
879	500	Blue Green–vy. dk. (1 strand)
215	320	Pistachio Green–med.
387	822	Beige Gray–lt.
942	738	Tan–vy. lt.
311	3827	Golden Brown–pale
373	422	Hazel Nut Brown–lt.
888	3828	Hazel Nut Brown
309	435	Brown–vy. lt.
371	433	Brown–med.
1014	3830	Terra Cotta
376	842	Beige Brown–vy. lt.
378	841	Beige Brown–lt.
899	3782	Mocha Brown–lt.
905	3781	Mocha Brown–dk.
397	3072	Beaver Gray–vy. lt.
900	648	Beaver Gray–lt.

Step 2: Backstitch (1 strand)

387	712	Cream
307	783	Christmas Gold
308	782	Topaz–med.
1019	3802	Antique Mauve–deep
101	327	Antique Violet–vy. dk.
894	223	Shell Pink–med.
896	3722	Shell Pink
78	3803	Mauve–dk.
101	550	Violet–vy. dk.
119	333	Blue Violet–vy. dk.
872	3740	Antique Violet–dk.
922	930	Antique Blue–dk.
149	336	Navy Blue
851	924	Slate Green–vy. dk.
1068	3808	Turquoise–ultra vy. dk.
844	3012	Khaki Green–med.
843	3364	Pine Green
862	3362	Pine Green–dk.
862	935	Avocado Green–dk.
862	934	Black Avocado Green
898	611	Drab Brown–dk.
380	839	Beige Brown–dk.
382	3371	Black Brown
905	3781	Mocha Brown–dk.
393	3790	Beige Gray–ultra vy. dk.

Step 3: French Knot (1 strand)

891	676	Old Gold–lt.
307	783	Christmas Gold
75	604	Cranberry–lt.
95	554	Violet–lt.
158	747	Sky Blue–vy. lt.
940	3807	Cornflower Blue
393	3790	Beige Gray–ultra vy. dk.

Step 4: Long Stitch (1 strand)

894	223	Shell Pink–med.
393	3790	Beige Gray–ultra vy. dk.

Step 5: Beadwork

00557 Gold

Top Left

Stitch Count: 117 width x 204 length

Top Right

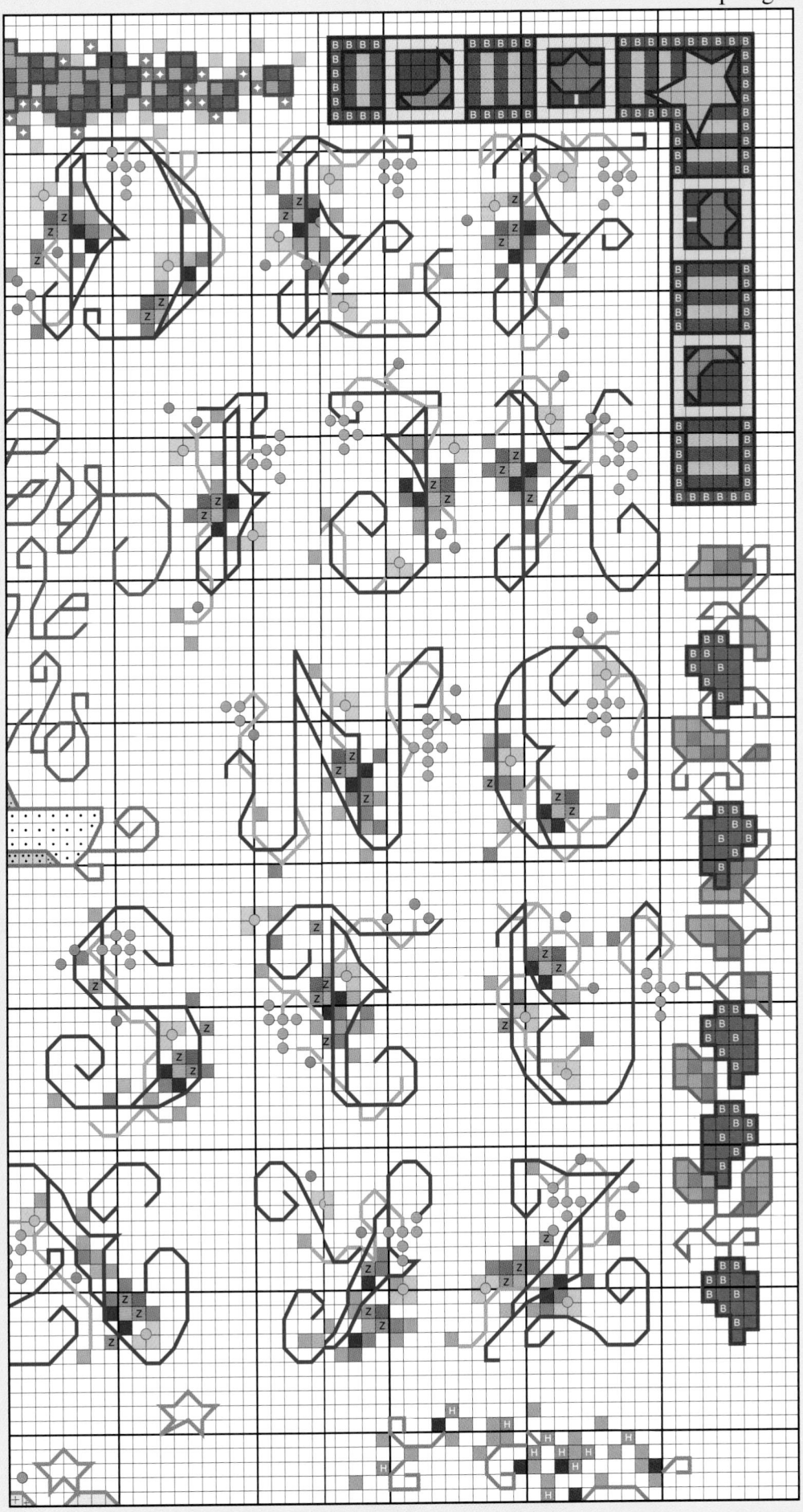

Bottom Left

Bottom Right

Metric Conversion Chart

mm-Millimetres cm-Centimetres

Inches to Millimetres and Centimetres

inches	mm	cm	inches	cm	inches	cm
⅛	3	0.3	9	22.9	30	76.2
¼	6	0.6	10	25.4	31	78.7
½	13	1.3	12	30.5	33	83.8
⅝	16	1.6	13	33.0	34	86.4
¾	19	1.9	14	35.6	35	88.9
⅞	22	2.2	15	38.1	36	91.4
1	25	2.5	16	40.6	37	94.0
1¼	32	3.2	17	43.2	38	96.5
1½	38	3.8	18	45.7	39	99.1
1¾	44	4.4	19	48.3	40	101.6
2	51	5.1	20	50.8	41	104.1
2½	64	6.4	21	53.3	42	106.7
3	76	7.6	22	55.9	43	109.2
3½	89	8.9	23	58.4	44	111.8
4	102	10.2	24	61.0	45	114.3
4½	114	11.4	25	63.5	46	116.8
5	127	12.7	26	66.0	47	119.4
6	152	15.2	27	68.6	48	121.9
7	178	17.8	28	71.1	49	124.5
8	203	20.3	29	73.7	50	127.0

Index

Alphabet Sampler, An 122
Animal Angels 80-86
Bear Angel 83
Bunny Angel 83
Kitten Angel 86
Puppy Angel 80
Squirrel Angel 80
Angel & Baby 88
Bear Sampler, A 116
Cathedral Glass 7
Celestial Melody 12
Cherubic Garden 15
Christmas Play, The 57
Christmas Sampler, A 97
Family Tree 92
Floral Sampler, A 103
General Instructions 4-5
Good Report, A 62
Jesus & the Children 31
Kids Count 71
Last Supper, The 43
Lion & the Lamb, The 49
Little Red Church 94
Mary & the Christ Child 27
Morning Chorus 89
Noah's Ark 53
Praying Child, A 62
Road to Bethlehem, The 21
Santa 66
Scenes of the Nativity 35
Scripture Reading 65
Three Wise Men 24
Two by Two 75
Winter Sampler, A 109